The Sea Bright Skiff
and Other Jersey Shore Boats

The Sea Bright Skiff

and Other Jersey Shore Boats

by Peter J. Guthorn

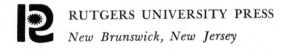

RUTGERS UNIVERSITY PRESS
New Brunswick, New Jersey

Acknowledgments

My original manuscript of 750 words was read by Mr. Kenneth H. Creveling, Director of the Department of Economic Development and Conservation, and Mr. Robert C. Campbell of the Newark *Star-Ledger,* both of whom encouraged my further research and writing. The ultimate encouragement and aid was from Mr. William Sloane of the Rutgers University Press.

Between the start and completion of the manuscript, isolated facts and fragments were obtained from a great number of individuals and sources, which are indicated in each chapter. I am particularly indebted to Mr. Wayne B. Yarnall, Mr. L. Albertson Huber, Mr. John Dubois, Mr. Harry Van Sant, Mr. Harold Seaman, and Mr. Joseph Banfield. Mr. Yarnall and Mr. Huber have been collectors of New Jersey marine history and lore for many years, their private collections having preserved a great deal of irreplaceable primary source material from oblivion. They both share with the others a vast and accurate memory, an aversion to folklore, accurate technical appraisal, and a deep interest. The builders' knowledge and experience is far beyond their immediate geographical area and immediate boat or vessel type.

The historical search was aided by Mr. Donald A. Sinclair's many suggestions for sources of data in the Rutgers University Library's Special Collections, and elsewhere. Mr. David Munn of the New Jersey State Library aided in suggesting additional sources of data, and searching out other reference material.

Other informants with particularly specialized knowledge contributed much data, and a viewpoint of experience, in their own field. These were Mr. William D. Wilkinson on lifeboats, Mr. John M. Kochiss of the Marine Historical Association on oysters, and Mr. John L. Lochhead of the Mariners Museum on general maritime historical sources.

The major part of the research was carried out in the New Jersey State Library, the Rutgers University Library, the Princeton University Library, the Monmouth County Historical Association Library, the Newark Public Library, The New Jersey Historical Society Library, the American Philosophical Society Library, and the National Archives. Additional local data were obtained from the files of the *Asbury Park Press,* and from Mr. Thomas Tighe of that newspaper.

Contents

I The Sea Bright Skiff

1

The Sea Bright Beach Skiffs

The exposed and unbroken beachline of northern Monmouth County was the birthplace of the New Jersey sea skiff or sea dory. It was later called the Sea Bright skiff, although its development antedated the town.

Beneath the Navesink Highlands, the beaches run south from Sandy Hook and the entrance to New York Harbor. The sea in summer is usually calm with a westerly breeze. The wind veers to the southeast during hot summer afternoons, bringing short, steep seas. Autumnal northeast storms are severe, and very destructive if lasting more than a day. Fall and spring storms arise rapidly and may carry snow or sleet, and fogs rival those of New England. Shark River, the first refuge, is twenty miles south of the Hook, Manasquan Inlet another six miles, and Barnegat Inlet twenty-four miles farther down the coast. All the inlets are treacherous in storms and nearly impassable in a northeaster. These exacting conditions shaped the development of the sea skiff as an able and safe boat for launching and landing through the surf.

During the second quarter of the nineteenth century New York's

population was increased by waves of immigrants, many from Catholic
countries. Fish catches in the waters about the city were insuffi-
cient, encouraging development of fisheries in New Jersey. The first
shore-fishing community was Nauvoo, which started about 1845 near
the present Sea Bright. Some years later the fishing community of
Galilee developed, close to the site of the present Monmouth Beach
Coast Guard station. A third beach-fishing center was in Long Branch
near the foot of Troutman Avenue.

Nauvoo and Galilee consisted of clusters of rough fishermen's
shacks, ice houses, fishing gear, boats, and related material. The picturesque communities so intrigued artists and journalists that they
were frequently pictured and described in contemporary popular magazines as early as 1857. These articles and illustrations are interesting
but not sufficiently accurate to add much useful knowledge.

The beach fisheries were very successful, each eventually having
from fifty to seventy-five skiffs. Skiff fishing employed bright metal or
painted squids jigged near the bottom, or by chumming with chopped
menhaden while using hooks baited with the same. Bluefish, mackerel,
and sea bass were caught commonly. Catches were large, the most productive grounds being the Shrewsbury Rocks, although areas farther
offshore, and north and south, were worked. The catch was brought
ashore every day, cleaned, packed, iced, and dispatched promptly to
the New York market by sloop or steamboat. The season was May to
November, although there was limited winter cod fishing.

The conical-roofed ice houses were seventy-five to one hundred
feet in circumference and fourteen feet deep. The bottom was eight
feet below ground level. The walls were insulated by banking with
sand, sawdust or tanbark. They cost $200 in 1880 and their capacity
was 150 to 200 tons of ice. Ice was cut during the winter from fresh-
water ponds or the nearby river. Each ice house could supply the needs
of four two-man fishing crews. They were frequently used jointly.
Occasionally the ice was exhausted before the end of the season, and
fishing was discontinued, as imported ice was too expensive.

In the Long Branch area in 1850, sixty-three proprietors were
engaged in fishing. Each had two to four employees, boats, seines, and

other equipment. The annual income reported was from $550 to
$1,000. In the late 1880's, individual incomes were as high as $12,000
to $15,000 a season. The fisherman bore typical New Jersey family
names like Wooley, Ridley, Warner, West, McLean, White, Disbrow,
Tallman, Lippincott, and Cooper. One man named Hennessey was
born in Ireland. A beach fishery and fish house had been established
at the site of the present Spring Lake by 1859.

The early beach skiffs were about 15 feet in length and 5 feet
beam. They had round bilges, a sloping transom, slightly rockered
plank keel and a marked sheer to the topsides. The hull was lap-
straked with white cedar over sawn frames. Fastenings were copper
rivets or clinch nails. Each plank was fastened to its mate at short
intervals to make a flexible, water-tight skin. The U-shaped transom
was raked about 30 degrees. The garboards were fastened to the stern
post vertically, below the transom. This produced a reverse chine at
the after end and a planked-up skeg. The wide-bottom plank with
tapered ends provided a resting surface when beached, while its rocker
made turning easy. The bottom plank was a third of the beam in
earlier models but some builders favored wider or narrower proportions. The sawn frames of cedar or oak crooks were replaced by steam-
bent white oak in later boats. The skiffs were rowed, or sailed with a
spritsail and jib. When under sail, steering was by an oar in a transom
notch, thole pins on the quarter, or rope loop. Rudders were rare.
There was a small centerboard or daggerboard. The light, buoyant,
flexible hulls were excellent surf boats. Photographs taken in 1872 of
the *Lizzie,* a beach skiff built by Isaac or William Seaman, show the
characteristics of hull and rig.

The skiff has many features in common with the oyster skiffs and
Whitehall boats of the New York Harbor area. They are closely related
to the New Jersey wrecking and life-saving skiffs discussed in the
chapter on surf boats, sometimes referred to as square-sterned whale
boats. They undoubtedly developed for both fishing and wrecking
at the same time.

The earliest recorded boat builders in the Long Branch area
were William Morris and Edwin Dennis, who were working by 1850.

In the next twenty years, H. C. Lane, Robert Emery, and Jesse Laber built skiffs in the same area. The principal builders during the last quarter of the century were Charles P. Huff, Lawrence B. Newman, Abram Joralemon, and Walter and William Seaman. The last named introduced the term "sea skiff" in an advertisement as early as 1885.

The output of each builder was small, from two to four yearly. Seaman and Joralemon built many small sailboats, launches, and other craft, while Huff and Newman limited their work to beach skiffs and surf boats. The design of each builder was characteristic. Huff's had a wider bottom, Newman's more flare to the topsides, and Seaman's had a fuller midship section. A few were constructed by fishermen, who, if successful, later became builders.

Builders of similar beach skiffs and surf boats worked in other communities during the same period. Those known and recognized were Jacob Herbert and A. Hanaway of Manasquan, R. A. Clark of Point Pleasant, Jacob Vaughn of Forked River, William Clock of Port Monmouth and William A. Douglas of Riceville.

After 1880 the beach skiffs increased to about 17 feet in length. Pound net fishing was becoming very productive, and skiffs were developed particularly for that use. During the last years of the century, many Scandinavian sailors left their vessels in New York for a summer of fishing. Some stayed, adding their names to the roster of Monmouth County's early commercial fishermen.

The beach skiff is still produced in its original form and size as a life-guard patrol and utility boat by Charles Hankins and Sons of Lavalette. The design and scantlings are almost identical to those built more than a century ago, except that they are no longer equipped with a centerboard or sails.

SOURCES

Publications

Goode, G. Brown *et al. The Fishing Industry of the United States.* Washington, D.C., 1887.

Schenck, J. H. *A Complete Descriptive Guide of Long Branch, N.J.* New York, 1868.

Beers, F. W. *Atlas of Monmouth County, New Jersey.* New York, 1873.

Rose, T. F., and H. C. Woolman. *Historical and Biographical Atlas of the New Jersey Coast.* Philadelphia, 1878.
Wolverton, Chester. *Atlas of Monmouth County, New Jersey.* New York, 1889.
Kobbe, Gustav. *The New Jersey Coast and Pines.* Short Hills, 1889.
McCutcheon, E. T. *Monmouth County Directory.* Newark, 1885.

Unpublished Material

New Jersey Census Records for 1850 and 1860. New Jersey State Library, Trenton

Personal Reminiscences and Anecdotal Material

Harold A. Seaman, Port-au-Peck
Joseph E. Banfield, Ocean Township
Herman A. Bennett, Spring Lake Heights
Oskar Kristensen, Asbury Park

The earliest known graphic representation of a Sea Bright-type skiff is a water color, "Fish Landing: Long Branch, N.J.," made by William Mason in 1834. The two skiffs at the left of the picture have a sloping transom, lap-strake construction, flat-bottom plank, and a reverse chine aft between garboard and second or "tuck" strake. *Courtesy of the Henry Francis du Pont Winterthur Museum.*

William A., Isaac, and Walter A. Seaman in the *Lizzie* at Nauvoo. Note spritsail rig, balanced jib club, steering oar. From a tintype made in 1872. *Courtesy of Harold A. Seaman.*

The *Lizzie* being launched from the beach. *Courtesy of Harold A. Seaman.*

The *Lizzie* under oars, sail stowed.
Courtesy of Harold A. Seaman.

A Seaman beach skiff being delivered,
about 1890.

Hankins Sea Bright Dory Surf Boat

Charles Hankins & Sons

BOAT BUILDERS SINCE 1912

Highway No. 35 - Lavallette, N. J.

Phone: 793-7443

An ideal general utility surf boat designed and built for rugged use offshore by sport fishermen, lifesavers and commercial men, from Maine to Florida. Easily handled and easily maintained. Excellent for surf launching.

Specifications:

Length O. A. 16'.

Beam 5'3".

Draught 1'.

Planking, $\frac{1}{2}$" white cedar lap streak.

Gunwales and caps, $1\frac{1}{2}$x$\frac{3}{4}$, white oak, one piece.

Stem and Stern Post, White Oak natural growth crook.

Transom, $1\frac{1}{4}$" cedar.

All Fastenings copper riveted, bronze and brass.

Two Pair Row Locks.

Famous Sea Bright Dory Surf Boat

Also Available As POWER SURF BOAT

This advertisement appeared about 1950. Specifications and construction of these skiffs are essentially unchanged after a century.

Three views of a Campbell beach skiff built about 1920.

Half hull of a Campbell beach skiff, about 1895.

2

Pound Fisheries and Pound Boats

The pound net is a fish trap constructed of a system of staked or fixed nets, in shore waters. They were first introduced into New Jersey in 1855 by George Snedeker of Gravesend, Long Island, and the first nets were set up in the shallow waters on the inner side of Sandy Hook.

Pound nets did not come into general use until 1873 due to the high initial investment. A pound net was established near Barnegat Inlet in 1878. By the following year, there were six between Long Branch and Sandy Hook, each clearing $7,000 yearly. One net lift in 1878 produced 3,500 pounds of fish valued at $700. By 1880 there were eleven nets between Long Branch and Sandy Hook, accounting for half of the total fish production. The number continued to increase to about twenty-five fisheries, each with from three to six pound nets, by the mid-1920's. The main varieties caught were weakfish, butterfish, bluefish, and bonito. Many other varieties were caught in small numbers including large sharks, ocean sunfish, and giant tuna. In one net haul at the Point Pleasant fishery, sixteen tuna from 300 to 980 pounds were taken.

The earliest pound nets were quite simple. Those in the shallower waters of Sandy Hook Bay had two heart-shaped bays which directed the fish into a pocket through a short funnel. The nets were suspended between poles without need for a horizontal mesh floor. The early offshore installations were similar to those to be described later. They were much smaller and rarely were in waters deeper than thirty feet. Another type, the submarine pound, was used occasionally between the World Wars. This vastly enlarged fyke was anchored to the sea floor and suspended by buoys and spars.

The later pound net was a complex and sophisticated development which had been improved, bit by bit, over a century. It consisted of a weir, forbay net, funnel, and a pocket net. The weir, or leader, was 900 feet long and was suspended on poles at right angles to the beach. The inshore end was 1,540 feet from the low-water mark on the beach. The weir was made of ½-inch manila lines, vertically suspended at progressively smaller intervals seaward. The intervals at the shore end were 8 inches, 6 inches in the central portion, and 4 inches or less in the 50 feet leading to the forbay. The weir was made in 70-foot sections except for the forbay end which was 50 foot. The vertical ½-inch lines were secured to 2-inch manila at top and bottom. The 2-inch top and bottom cables were continuous at the ends, forming a quadrilateral vertical grid of rope. The top rope was fastened at short intervals to a ¼-inch, 7-strand, galvanized cable, suspended above high water between pound poles at 70-foot intervals. The 2-inch bottom cable was secured at short intervals to a ⅞- or 1-inch iron chain on the sea floor. The top cable was secured to the poles with manila line which could be easily cut in an emergency.

The funnel-shaped forbay was made of 3-inch mesh, suspended horizontally on poles and guys, from sea floor to above high water. It was made of 35-foot sections and had recurved ends at the shoreward side, forming a rough heart shape. The seaward end of the forbay was 40 feet wide, entering the funnel. The funnel net tapered to 8 feet where it entered the pocket, several feet below low-water level. The pocket was the final receptacle for the fish. It was 50 feet square, made of 2½-inch net, and suspended on guys above high-water level.

The weir was supported on thirteen or fourteen poles, the forbay on ten, and the pocket nine poles for support. The later pound nets

were expensive to build and maintain. They were particularly liable
to extensive storm damage. Manila rope and cable were purchased by
the ton. Pound poles were as long as 90 feet and 30 inches at the butt
end. The cost of a completed pound was as much as $15,000 in 1960.
Additional investment was required for the pound boats, shore packing
station, and ice house.

The pound fisheries decreased in numbers following World War
II and were abandoned in 1961. Production had diminished so that a
single pound boat was sufficient to service three nets, where formerly
a boat had been required for each. Prior to 1940 there were large
pound fisheries at Seaside Park, Chadwick, Mantoloking, Bay Head,
Point Pleasant, Manasquan, Spring Lake, Bradley Beach, Deal, El-
beron, Long Branch, Monmouth Beach, Sea Bright, and within Sandy
Hook Bay. Other fisheries were at Long Beach Island, Sea Isle City,
and on Five Fathom Bank off Cape May, as well as Delaware Bay.

The placing of pound net poles was a difficult task unless the sea
was absolutely flat. Two pound boats were secured together catamaran
fashion, using heavy timbers athwart both, leaving a gap between the
hulls. The poles were directed downward to the sandy bottom where
they were washed in with a powerful water jet. The jet was directed
through a 20-foot section of 2-inch pipe, lashed to a cedar pole of sufficient length to reach bottom. Long timbers and a lot of muscle were
required where pound poles were put in water of depths to 62 feet.

During the most productive years, before World War II, individual
pounds produced an average of 300,000 to 400,000 pounds of fish a
season, and some as much as 600,000 pounds or more. The Point Pleasant fishery produced as much as 100,000 pounds from its several nets
in one day.

Scandinavian fishermen, mostly Swedish, were attracted to the
shore fisheries during the latter years of the last century. They were
well received because of their skill and hardihood. They soon pros-
pered, eventually dominating the pound net fisheries.

During the early years of pound net fishing, the ordinary beach
skiff was used. It was gradually enlarged and modified for pound net
use, reaching a length of 20 to 24 feet by 1900. The crew consisted of

six rowers and a captain. The rowers used 12-foot ash oars through thole pins and the captain a 15- to 18-foot sweep for steering, through a transom notch or thole pins. In the early years, the captain was a surfman and not a fisherman. He was responsible for getting the boat, crew and fish intact through the surf. The crew manned the oars and emptied or repaired net and gear without orders from the captain. The skilled Swedish sailors displaced the superspecialist surfman, as they could handle both responsibilities.

The first practical engine for marine use was developed before 1900 and was employed in pound boats by 1907 or 1908. It did not entirely supplant oars for another four or five years. Power encouraged an increase in size, 30-foot boats becoming common by 1910. The hull design, with planked-up skeg and horizontal bottom plank, permitted the engine and shaft to remain horizontal. This was a necessity in the days of splash lubrication.

The rudder replaced the steering oar in the power pound boats. It hung outboard in a vertical position against the sloping transom. The lower pintle was supported by a heavy tripod strut of 1-inch round iron, or by a 1-by-2-inch iron shoe projecting from the bottom of the skeg. Later, a rudder of iron plate welded on a $2\frac{1}{2}$-inch iron rudder post was used. The upper end of the post passed through the transom and was controlled by an inboard tiller. This design was introduced by Seaman, and widely adapted.

In the early power boats, the engine was housed between thwartships watertight bulkheads. Fuel tanks were in the same compartment, on each side of the engine, the whole covered by removable covers. The flywheel protruded through the forward bulkhead for hand starting. The 2-cycle engines with make-and-break ignition could be reversed by the experienced operator. The ignition switch was opened, then closed just before the engine reached dead center. A 25-foot pound boat could be propelled at 4 or 5 knots by a 10- to 12-horsepower 2-cycle engine. They were almost completely superseded by the more powerful and economical 4-cycle engine by 1914. By this time, the engine was housed in a watertight box-shaped compartment beneath the helmsman's platform aft.

There was a further increase in size following the war. In 1932, Seaman offered standard pound boats in sizes 32 by 10, 36 by 11 and 42 by 12 feet. The cost of the finished hull alone was respectively $960, $1,860 and $2,990. The details of construction are covered in another chapter.

The carrying capacity of the average 30-foot pound boat was 12 to 15 tons, depending on sea and weather. The capacity of a 40- or 42-foot boat was up to 25 tons. A pair of very large boats were built by Banfield about 1925 for the Live Fish Co. of Islip, Long Island. These were of ordinary proportions but were 54 feet long. They were built with double keelsons and the thwarts were nearly 6 feet above the bottom. They were very successful but no more of like size were built. They were not launched through the surf but were used to transfer fish from pound net to live enclosure, or from enclosure to packing shed.

The most commonly used engine from 1930 on was the Model A Ford automobile conversion. The conversion was often minimal, omitting water-jacketed exhaust manifold. Also used were the standard 4-cylinder, 4-cycle marine engines developing from 40 to 60 horsepower. The popular makes were the Mianus, Palmer, and Kermath. A reverse gear was usual and the shaft turned a 3-bladed wheel. In earlier boats, 2-bladed propellers were used. The shaft was marked so that the blades could be put into a horizontal position when beaching, protective skegs not having come into use.

Efficient gear was needed for beaching and launching, especially as size increased. Temporary ramps of heavy planking were laid to the surf. Locust rollers were used beneath the keel and propulsion was furnished by a team of horses hooked to the boat through an intermediate 2-wheeled sulky. After the boat was in the surf, it was hauled off by a heavy line secured to a piling off the beach. This was formerly done by the crew, hauling hand over hand. Later, the engine was geared to drive an upright pulley or power head forward of the engine box. A couple of turns of the hauling line about it relieved the crew of this heavy task.

Beaching the returning boat was much harder. The now heavily laden boat had to be hauled through the surf and up the inclined beach. Heavy iron straps were fastened outside the rub strakes in the forward quarter of the hull. These were bolted through the frames and formed a ring at the stem. The ring provided a place to hook the hauling line. Others had a 3-inch iron eye inserted through the stem in the lower third. This was continued inboard, being attached to the keel and keelson by a 1-inch tie rod. Some later boats abandoned the rockered bottom plank for one that was flat, to facilitate hauling. In late years, tractors replaced teams, and occasionally windlasses were used. Also, some pound fisheries used inlets and dockage, rather than beaching. This was possible and practical for the faster boats servicing pounds near passable inlets.

Fish were unloaded from the beached boat by shoveling them into two-handled baskets, of thin oak slats, holding 50 pounds. The baskets were manufactured in New Egypt, New Jersey, and elsewhere by manufacturers of agricultural baskets. They were dipped in pine pitch before use, as a binder and preservative. The filled baskets were racked on a wagon, for hauling to the fish shed. Here they were sorted and packed into 50-gallon wood barrels. A layer of crushed ice was placed in the bottom, followed by alternating layers of fish and ice. The barrel was topped off by a final layer of ice and covered by a piece of sacking. Fragile fish, such as butterfish, had water added to the barrel to minimize bruising. The barrels held about 200 pounds of fish. They were transported by train to New York markets, for sale by commission merchants. Rarely, fish were sent to Philadelphia or other cities. In later years truck transportation was increasingly used.

The pound fishery shore station consisted of a sorting and packing shed, ice house, living quarters, and facilities for repair of equipment.

Fisheries had abandoned cutting and storing their own ice by the end of the century. Locally manufactured ice was available so only a two- or three-day supply was kept on hand. Quarters for the unmarried crew was a bunkhouse or loft above the packing shed. This included a galley and eating area. Some fishery crews did their own cooking but most had a full-time cook. Wages at the turn of the century were $30 monthly, with food. This was twice the pay of seamen on many foreign vessels. Separate cabins were provided for married men, most of whom had children.

Fishing gear saw hard service. Torn nets were replaced and

repaired ashore. Nets and lines required dipping in preservatives and antifouling compounds at four- to six-week intervals. Pine tar, green copper, and red copper compounds were used in large amounts. Long racks for drying and large receptacles for dipping were required as sections were several hundred feet in length.

A shop for engine repair, service for shafts, propellers, other machinery, and iron fishing gear required a mechanic who could double as blacksmith. A gallows or sheer legs was used to haul out and replace engines.

The more remote fisheries before World War I were quite complete and self-sufficient communities. Many tended to lose their identity as the surrounding areas grew up. Some were spread over quite large acreage, purchased for very little. Resale in recent years was very profitable.

The pound boats were impressive out of proportion to their size. The strong sheer, fine proportions, excellent workmanship and generous dimensions of their wood members made them seem larger and more imposing. The landing of a loaded boat through a heavy surf was an exciting experience which never failed to attract many onlookers. The picturesque complex of shore station, fishing boats, and pound net offshore has completely disappeared.

SOURCES

Publication

Goode, G. Brown *et al. The Fishing Industry of the United States.* Washington, D.C., 1887.

Personal Reminiscences and Anecdotal Material

Joseph E. Banfield, Ocean Township
Herman A. Bennett, Spring Lake Heights
Axel B. Carlson, Jr., Manasquan
Harold A. Seaman, Port-au-Peck
George C. C. Wilson, South Belmar
Oskar Kristensen, Asbury Park

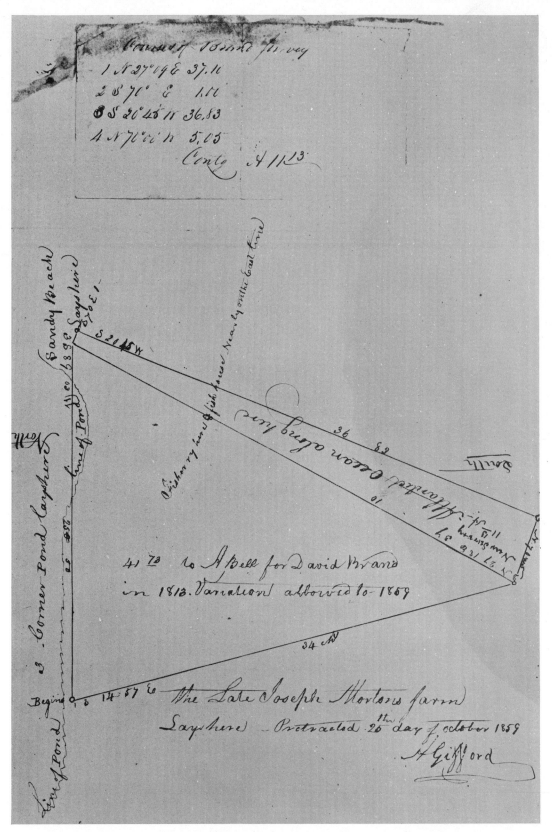

An 1859 survey of the area of present-day Spring Lake, showing location of the fishery and fish house. *Courtesy of Robert L. White.*

Twenty-four-foot rowing pound boat, owned by Gus Wooley's fishery at Spring Lake, 1907. *Courtesy of Axel B. Carlson, Jr.*

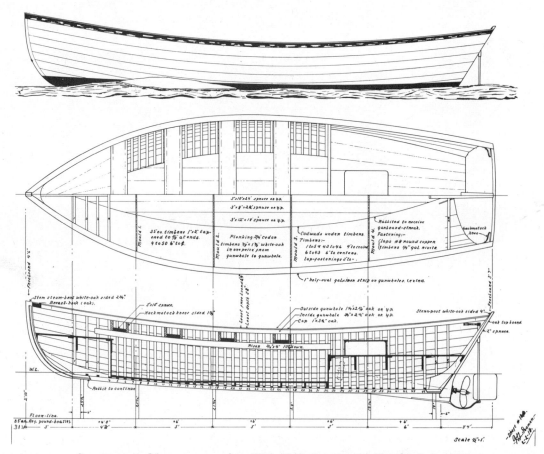

Seaman pound boat construction, 1918–1940. *Courtesy of Harold A. Seaman.*

Data from a boat builder's notebook. Comparison of sections of 35-foot pound boats as constructed by L. B. Newman and Harold A. Seaman. *Courtesy of Harold A. Seaman.*

SEAMAN SEA BRIGHT SEA SKIFFS

The choice of PROFESSIONAL DEEP SEA FISHERMEN since their origination at "NAUVOO" (now SEA BRIGHT, N. J.)
by Walter A. Seaman in 1841

● Owing to their lightness, stability, surf-carrying capacity, and their ability to land through the surf and skid out on the beach and sit upright when aground they are ideal for tenders, life-boats, bathing-beach rescue-boats, cargo-boats, lighters or any other use requiring exceptional sea-boats capable of carrying exceptional loads through the SURF.

We have reports of 21 footers landing over 5,600 pounds of fish through the surf and 20,000 pounds is not exceptional for the 32 footers. These boats are pulled out of the surf on rollers with their load and stand up under this treatment year after year.

36' x 11' SEA-SKIFF POUND-BOAT
Used by Pound-net Fishermen for use off and on the beach through the surf.

36' x 11' SEA-SKIFF
(Pound - Net Boat)

Overhang stern with fishermans Rudder

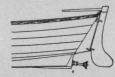

Regular stern with fishermans Rudder

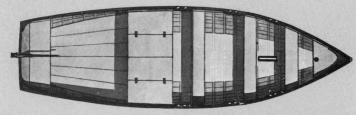

STANDARD SIZES

Overhang Stern		Regular Stern
$ 590.	16'x5'	$ 490.
690.	18'x6'	590.
790.	21'x6'9"	690.
990.	26'x8'	890.
1,890.	32'x11'	1,690.
2,190.	36'x11'	1,990.

P R I C E S   A R E
for complete Skiffs (as cuts) ready to receive power.

W E   I N S T A L L
any make of motor or equipment desired at the prevailing prices.

P R I C E S   A R E
subject to change without notice. Orders are accepted contingent upon strikes, fires, accidents, delays by carriers or any cause beyond our control.

21' REGULATION SEA-SKIFF
Used by Professional fishermen for use off and on the beach through the surf.

TELEPHONE L. B. 3495   *S EAMAN EA-SKIFFS*   LONG BRANCH, N. J.

1841   —   PIONEER BUILDERS OF THE FAMOUS SEA BRIGHT SEA - SKIFF   —   To Date

Seaman sales circular, about 1935.

Thirty-five-foot Seaman pound boat. *Courtesy of Harold A. Seaman.*

Seaman boat shop and a new pound boat. *Courtesy of Harold A. Seaman.*

Pound boat rudder.

Stern and bow of a late Hankins pound boat.

Fishermen's shanties, Galilee.

Pitch pot, Galilee.

Net racks and ramps, Galilee.

Packing shed,
Galilee.

Abandoned pound
boats.

Gus Wooley's Spring Lake fishery, 1907. *Courtesy of Axel B. Carlson, Jr.*

Gus Wooley's packing shed, 1907. *Courtesy of Axel B. Carlson, Jr.*

Galilee fishery and beached boats, wagons, and teams, about 1925. St. Peter's Church in background.

Chadwick fishery, engine gallows, sheds, crew's quarters, and gear.

Point Pleasant fishery packing shed, about 1945. *Courtesy of Axel B. Carlson, Jr.*

Washing in pound poles, using Gould pump and 6-H.P. Mianus engine, 1905. *Courtesy of Harold A. Seaman.*

Pound fishing boat offshore, 1938. *Asbury Park Press.*

Unloading a pound boat, 1938. *Asbury Park Press.*

Pound boat with a large catch of cod, Point Pleasant fishery, 1945. *Carlson Photos*.

3

Other Fishing Types

The pound fisheries accounted for the major portion of the fish caught. However, other types of fishing were practiced along the New Jersey coast. Later, specially adapted Sea Bright skiffs were employed, and some further refined.

Lobstering, gill netting, and seine netting were carried on in the early years, all using the early type of beach skiff.

The Atlantic lobster fishery extended as far south as Atlantic City. Lobstering was carried on off the shore between Sea Bright and Long Branch as early as 1860, primarily for local consumption. Catches declined to 1870, but began to pick up two years later, increasing to 1880. In 1880 there were fourteen boats engaged exclusively in lobstering, each with a two-man crew. The production was 156,000 pounds valued at $5,488.

Each boat set thirty to forty traps, in rocky spots at depths from five to eleven fathoms. The crew passed the day hand-line fishing, retrieving the traps later in the day. The average catch was 140 pounds daily, of lobsters weighing from $1\frac{1}{4}$ to $1\frac{3}{4}$ pounds. A newly designed pot of netting supported on a frame of three hoops was introduced by

Charles Woolley of Sea Bright in 1872, and largely superseded the older lath pot.

Gill netting was used almost exclusively for bluefish, later being employed for mackerel, weakfish and others. Nets of $3\frac{1}{2}$- to 4-inch mesh, 100 fathoms long, were used offshore between August and November. When the nets were set out in a straight line, the catch was solely bluefish. About 1873, it was discovered that sharp angles in the set of the net produced catches of mackerel. This produced arrangements similar to the pound net, the common sets being the square, "T" and harpoon. The production of each set averaged about $400 but ran as high as $1,092.

Seine netting was more commonly used in the rivers and bays, less commonly offshore. There was an extensive winter rock and perch fishery at Metedeconk Neck at the northern end of Barnegat Bay. In 1880 this employed 196 men with forty-nine seines from November to April. Seines were hauled in open water and also under the ice. A single haul of 80,000 pounds was reported about 1850, and 15,000 to 25,000 pounds could be taken daily by a single net. The total catch in the winter 1879–80 was over 500,000 pounds valued at $36,700. There was some limited spring herring fishing as well.

The introduction of power about 1907 increased the fisherman's operating radius. Under oars and sail they could cover up to thirty miles in a day. Power doubled this, and left more time and energy for fishing. The development of skiffs for lobstering, gill netting, and seining proceeded, the boats being usable for all types of offshore work. There were some minor differences in the gear required, but gill nets or seines could be payed out over the stern of a slowly moving boat, as well as a line of lobster pots.

Gill netting from surf-launched skiffs was practiced progressively farther south, after the introduction of power. Chumming with ground bait was used increasingly, often off an established pound net, which in itself was an attraction to fish. After a school had been attracted by chumming, the net was dropped about them. Occasionally, the school had to be spooked by towing an anchor through them, to cause a run into the nets. Gill netters consistently brought home fish, the quantity varying from 1,000 to 12,000 pounds daily. A good average was 6,000 pounds.

Some of the gill net fishermen moved their operations to Florida in the winter, introducing many practices developed in New Jersey. One pioneer, who stayed in Fort Pierce, was Walter Peterson. They usually took a month to prepare their gear and boats. Before leaving, new boats were ordered for delivery the following spring. The boats and gear were then transported by Clyde-Mallory Line to Miami, or by train to Fort Pierce. In the latter case, the boats were then sailed, rowed, or cruised to Miami for the winter's fishing. The season was completed by April, and boats and gear were sold locally. The crews returned to their newly constructed skiffs for the coming fishing season in New Jersey. The migratory fishermen started this practice before 1890 and continued at least until World War I.

Other shore fishermen migrated for a month's shad fishing to the larger or smaller rivers of New Jersey, Delaware, Maryland, or Virginia. The traditional start was St. Patrick's Day. Other shore fishermen migrated to the Raritan River, the Hackensack, Hudson, Housatonic, and many others for the shad season.

Prior to 1914, the general utility Sea Bright skiff was 16- to 19-foot with a beam of 6- to 6½-foot. It was powered by an engine developing 20 to 30 horsepower. This was ordinarily used through the surf but an increasing number of fishermen abandoned the beach as an operating base for nearby inlets. The inlet-based skiff was slightly longer, comparatively narrower, but otherwise the same as the beach skiff. Average dimensions were length 21 feet and beam 6 to 6½ feet.

Two changes were made at this time, although not simultaneously, and not by all the builders. The freeboard was increased and sheer flattened. The rocker of the bottom plank and the sheer of the gunwales was diminished by about half. The objective of the builders is obvious, but speeds in excess of 10 or 12 miles per hour caused the stern to squat.

The next change was the application of horizontal planes of planking about the transom and stern to prevent settling as speed increased. The squat boards were partially effective. Some builders moved the engine and fuel tank forward of the center of buoyancy, which diminished seaworthiness but did not increase speed. It should be noted that almost every sea skiff had a small daggerboard forward, a practice continued until 1940. A square foot of lateral plane forward was a great aid in steering when trimmed by the stern, or with a beam wind.

The conventional rudder and tiller interfered with dropping a gill or seine net. This was solved by omitting the tiller and the upper quarter of the rudder stock. Steering lines were secured to the after end of the rudder. The steering lines were passed along the sides below the gunwales through chocks. The helmsman sat forward of the engine box, steering by the rudder lines. Most of these boats had a tiller with extension to control the rudder in conventional fashion when needed.

Another development was the overhanging stern. In order to overcome squatting, the transom had become wider, the bottom flatter, and the transom had lost much of its rake. The underwater portion of the hull was modified by projecting the stern 18 to 24 inches aft of the propeller. In the first overhanging stern models, an outboard fisherman-type rudder was used. This was replaced by a smaller spade rudder mounted beneath the transom through a watertight bearing and gland.

The overhanging transom was first introduced about 1916 and the spade rudder a year or two later. The tendency to widen and flatten the stern continued. With larger engines the better designed sea skiffs became semiplaning. A new development was the reversed bottom curve in the after third, patented by Stewart B. King of Highlands in 1920.

By the early 1920's there were four general types or varieties of the Sea Bright skiff. The beach skiff, many of substantial age, were 16 to 19 feet long. By this time, most were based in the inlets, although a few continued to be surf launched. The fishing skiff was 24 to 26 feet long, was somewhat newer and faster, was provided with steering lines run to the forward cockpit, and was adapted to gill netting. The lobstermen were 26 to 28 feet long, were still newer, faster, and had a vertical overhanging transom. The pound boats were 30 to 36 feet long, with limited speed but great carrying capacity, and were increasingly based in inlets. Each was adapted for a particular service but all were, to a limited extent, used interchangeably.

The lobster, or more correctly lobster service, boats were among the first to use a modified construction of the planked-up skeg. Initially this hollow appendage had been formed by the reverse curve of the after end of the garboards fastened in a vertical plane to a stern post. Now, with the horizontal transom and omission of the transom mounted rudder, greater stresses were exerted, causing leaking. The new construction consisted of a planked-up skeg formed of the bottom plank, and the sides by tapered planks rabbeted to the bottom plank below, and the edges of the horizontal garboards above. The stuffing box and stern bearing were secured to a triangular block at the after end of the appendage. This was the box garboard as contrasted to the earlier rolled garboard. The box garboard was adapted to the earlier design of beach skiff, but primarily to the later type of overhanging transom design. The latter required heavy horn timbers to maintain longitudinal strength and watertight integrity.

There were further refinements in design. Bottoms became flatter transversely and longitudinally while the box garboard appendage diminished in size. The box garboard had been omitted from some smaller skiffs in the 1930's, and progressively on larger boats, to its near complete abandonment by 1940. A contributing factor was the introduction of dry crankcase engines using pressure lubrication. The older horizontal crankcase engine, depending on splash lubrication, found the box or rolled garboard desirable. The new engine would operate well at an angle.

Twin-engine installations became increasingly popular as a means to increase power and speed at lower cost. Automobile engines were inexpensive and available. Counterrotation was not considered important. The additional reliability of dual installations became apparent. The ordinary practice was to replace one engine each year as the life of a Pierce Arrow, Packard, or Buick engine was about two years. The usual cause of failure was erosion or clogging of the head jackets. Most engines were prepared by circulating a mixture of red lead and linseed oil through the jackets before use at sea. Sometimes, when an engine was to be replaced, an exact match in make or size could not be found, no deterrent to the pragmatic fisherman.

By 1950, the skiff used for offshore work, lobstering or fishing, was about 28 feet long. It was employed interchangeably for all types of service with the exception of pound nets. Power was provided by a pair of V-8, counterrotating, marine conversions with fresh-water cooling. Oldsmobile engines were very popular but almost all makes gave excellent service. The total effective horsepower was 250 to 350, giving a service speed of 22 to 24 miles per hour with reasonable gas consumption. The stem tended to be straight and raked, freeboard forward was high, the sheer of the topsides less than on earlier models, and the stern low. There was more extensive decking forward and a closed shelter forward. Initially this had been a forward spray shield on a pipe frame. Sometimes this was only a shelter cabin or windshield. The cockpit floor was flat, extending from the shelter forward to the transom. Relieving ports were aft through the transom. The low profile of the V-8 engines made the flush deck possible. Engines were often exhausted through a stack. These boats were, and still are, comfortable, efficient, fast, and seaworthy. Unfortunately, they are too plain to appeal to the boating public.

It is possible to recapitulate the development of the Sea Bright skiff in a series of half models made by the Campbell family of Belmar. The first is typical of the rowing-sailing beach skiffs about 1900. It was built in 15 to 17 feet lengths by Neill Campbell whose average production was two or three yearly. The second was a higher-sided, somewhat flatter model for engines of 20 to 30 horsepower. It was built in lengths of 17 to 21 feet, with a beam of $6\frac{1}{4}$ feet, from 1915 to 1925, by Neill and his son Robert J. The third was a gill net and lobstering skiff introduced in 1936. This had an overhanging stern, nearly vertical transom, and box garboards. The standard size was $25\frac{1}{2}$ by $7\frac{1}{2}$ feet, but was built in lengths from 23 to 28 feet. It was designed for engines up to a total of 250 horsepower. One with 350 horsepower made 35 miles per hour. These models were built up to 1950.

The fourth is a skiff without box garboard or skeg. This hull was 20 by $6\frac{1}{2}$ feet and powered by one or two engines developing to 300 horsepower. These were capable of speeds to 42 miles per hour. Boats of this design were built by Neill Campbell's grandsons Robert D. and

Donald M. from 1946 to 1956. A number of Campbell skiffs are still in use, some dating back to World War I. As with most small boat shops, sales and service have replaced construction.

SOURCES

Publication

Goode, G. Brown *et al. The Fishing Industry of the United States.* Washington, D.C., 1887.

Personal Reminiscences and Anecdotal Material

Donald M. Campbell, Belmar
Robert D. Campbell, Belmar
Axel B. Carlson, Jr., Manasquan
Edward Gant, Glendola
Edmund L. Thompson, Jr., Neptune
Edgar A. Huff, Long Branch
Harry F. Lovgren, Sea Bright
Ensley M. White, Red Bank
Howard K. Hayden, Long Branch

Three views of a Joralemon utility skiff, 17 by 6 feet, built about 1905.

Skiffs on the beach at Sea Bright, about 1907. *Courtesy of Ensley M. White and Howard K. Hayden.*

Fishing skiffs on the beach at Sea Bright, 1908. This was the period of transition from oars and sails to power. *Courtesy of Ensley M. White and Howard K. Hayden.*

Landing through the surf, Sea Bright, about 1907. *Courtesy of Ensley M. White and Howard K. Hayden.*

Fishermen on the beach at Sea Bright about 1907. Note that the skiff has become a little larger and that a two-bladed propeller protrudes from the stern. The thole pins are still present. *Courtesy of Ensley M. White and Howard K. Hayden.*

Eighteen by six-foot Seaman skiff, 1915.

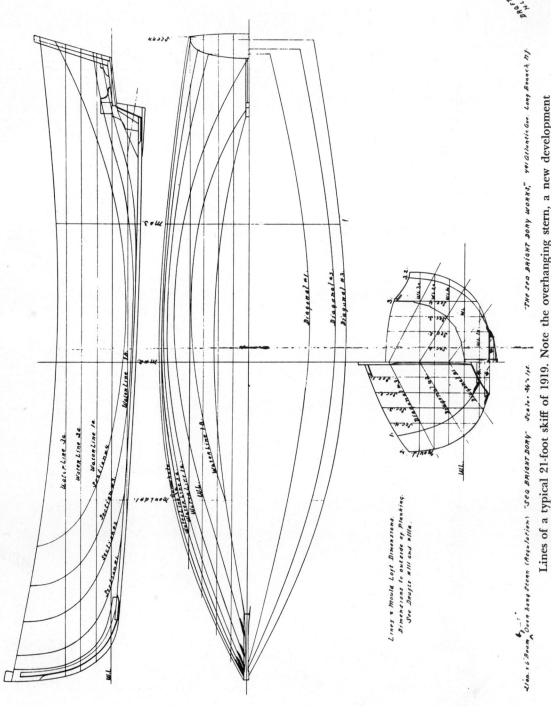

Lines of a typical 21-foot skiff of 1919. Note the overhanging stern, a new development in comparison with the earlier boats shown. *Courtesy of Harold A. Seaman.*

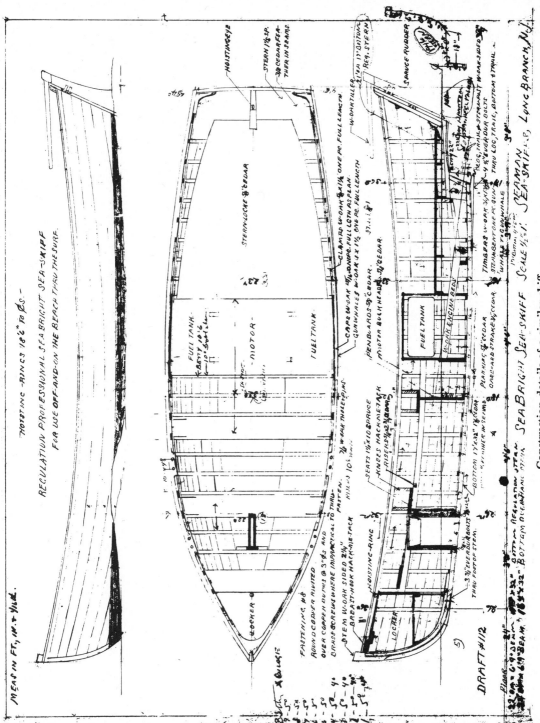

Construction details of a similar skiff.

KEYPORT BOAT WORKS
(on Main Highway to Asbury Park)

Business 'Phone KEYPORT 430   KEYPORT, N. J.   Residence 'Phone KEYPORT 919

Complete 26 Foot Sea Skiff De Luxe
a seaworthy runabout with a good turn of speed

SPECIFICATIONS

BEAM: 6' 8".
BOTTOM: 2" B. C. Spruce.
PLANKING: ⅝" Select White Cedar (lapstrake).
STEMPOST: 2" x 4" Steam Bent Oak.
STERNPOST: 4" Oak.
SKAG: 4" Spruce.
STERN TRANSOM: Spruce and Oak frame (seam battened covered with ¼" Mahogany).
FRAMES: ¾" x 1½" Oak (spaced 6" centers).
FASTENINGS: Copper rivets and brass screws.
BULKHEADS: Mahogany (varnished).
DECKS, COVERING BOARD AND GUNWALE: Mahogany (varnished).
FLOORS: ¾" White Cedar (T. & G. covered with Linoleum).
FLOOR HATCHES: Brass bound and fitted with flush Hatch Ring.
WINDSHIELD: Mahogany, plate glass sash, 2 hinged sash in forward panel and 2 stationary on each side. Top: laminated Fir covered with canvas.

ENGINE BOX: Mahogany, panelled sides. Flush top, hinged.
SEATS: 1 upholstered aft Lazy-Back.
EQUIPMENT: 1 brass combination Bit and Bow light, 1 hollow base stern cleat, 2 Stern Chocks, 2 Bow Chocks, 1 Folding Anchor (30-lb.) 60' of ¾" Anchor Rope, 1 Aft Flagpole Socket, 1 Flag, 1 Flagpole, 6 Life Preservers, Fog horn, Bell, and 1 Fire Extinguisher.
RUDDER: Columbia Speed Rudder (Brass).
STEERING WHEEL: Erico Kaïner Auto Type Drag Link Steerer.
PAINT: All bright wood is to be properly stained and varnished, 3 coats, all painted wood is to be given 3 coats of paint, color optional.
MOTOR INSTALLATION: All necessary fittings for a first-class installation, such as copper exhaust pipe, brass water fittings, Bronze Shaft, Hyde propeller, 1 30-gallon galvanized gasoline tank, Bronze stuffing box.
CONTROLS: All controls brought to forward bulkhead.

PRICES

Price of Hull without Engine $

PRICE COMPLETE WITH

		Speed	
Model F4	40-60 H.P. Scripps Marine Engine	18 M.P.H.	$
Model F6	100 H.P. Scripps Marine Engine	23 M.P.H.	$
Model G6	150 H.P. Scripps Marine Engine	30 M.P.H.	$

Prices on other engines furnished upon application.

---

26 Foot Open Type Sea Skiff

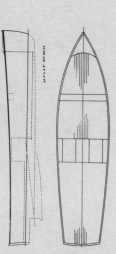

SPECIFICATIONS

L. O. A.: 26'.
BEAM: 6' 8".
BOTTOM: 2" Spruce (Sliptongued in Seams).
PLANKING: ⅝" Best Quality Select Grade White Cedar (Lapstrake).
FRAMES: ¾" x 1¼" Oak (Spaced 6" Centers).
FASTENINGS: Copper Rivets and Brass Screws.

FLOORS: ¾" White Cedar T. & G. Painted.
BULKHEADS: ¾" White Cedar T. & G. Painted.
FORWARD DECK AND LOCKER: ¾" White Cedar T. & G. Painted.
SEATS: 1 Hackmatack Kneed seat forward.
ENGINE BOX: ¾" White Cedar T. & G. Painted.
STEERER: 1 Skiff Steerer.
RUDDER: 1 Columbia High Speed Type.

PRICES

Price of Hull without Engine $

PRICE COMPLETE WITH

		Speed	
Model F4	40-60 H.P. Scripps Marine Engine	19 M.P.H.	$
Model F6	100 H. P. Scripps Marine Engine	24 M.P.H.	$
Model G6	150 H.P. Scripps Marine Engine	31 M.P.H.	$

Prices of other engines upon application.

We have been successfully building sea skiffs for the last seventeen years and we cordially invite your inspection of these models at our plant.

KEYPORT BOAT WORKS
(Just South of Perth Amboy on Main Highway to Asbury Park, N. J.)
Keyport, N. J.

Pages from the catalog of the Keyport Boat Works, operated by Kofoed, 1925. Note the excellent performance. *Courtesy of Harold Kofoed.*

Seaman skiff with overhanging stern, 1919. These boats all had a small centerboard forward. *Courtesy of Harold A. Seaman.*

A "chaser" built by Kofoed for the New Jersey Fish and Game Commission about 1930. Speed was 32 M.P.H.

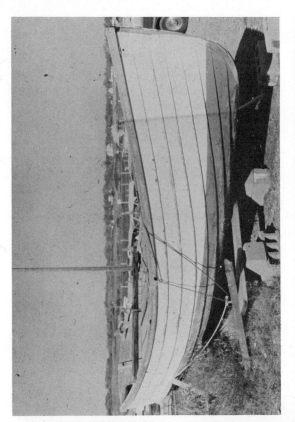
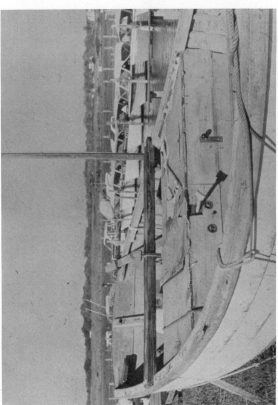
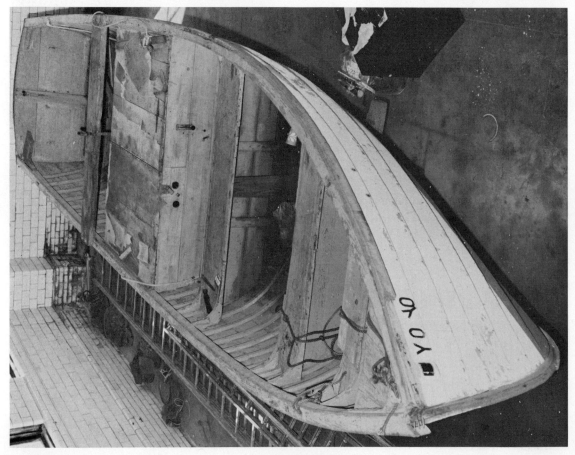

Views of a typical 24-foot utility skiff built from 1925 to 1935, with "squat boards" and steering lines.

Gant Brothers fishery on Shark River about 1946, one of the many similar bases for operations of gill netters, lobstermen, and purse seiners. Note large pile of lobster pots or fish traps in background, drying racks for nets at dockside, and seven lap-strake fishing skiffs, varying from about 24 to 28 feet in length. A sea skiff cabin cruiser is in the foreground. *Courtesy of Gant Brothers.*

Hauling a repaired net aboard a Gant Brothers utility skiff about 1950. Note the self-bailing after cockpit, parting boards, hand pump in the bilge, and decking over the engine compartment. *Courtesy of Gant Brothers.*

Hauling in gill net. Note the type of buoy used at the net ends, and the deep sea rod and reel. The Gants were not unwilling to fish for large tuna, bonita, or albacore when the opportunity was presented. *Courtesy of Gant Brothers.*

The Gant skiff was a 28-foot open model, powered by a 140-H.P. Chrysler engine. *Courtesy of Gant Brothers.*

Chumming gear: gasoline engine powered chum grinder, cans for holding ground and unground chum. One fisherman hand lining for large fish. *Courtesy of Gant Brothers.*

Hull of fast utility skiff built about 1950.

Utility skiff with forward house, loaded with lobster pots.

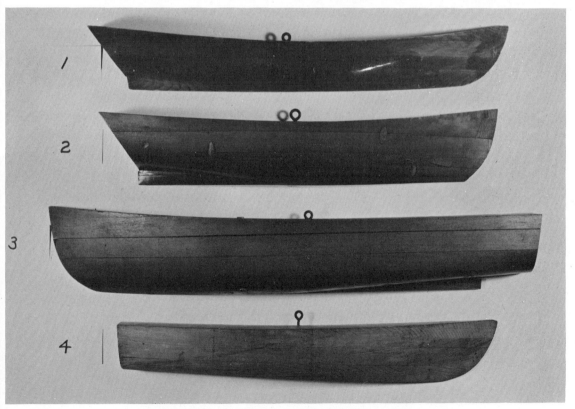

Skiff design recapitulation in Campbell half hulls.

4

Sea Bright Skiff Construction

There are many common features in the construction of the several types of Sea Bright skiff. As a point of departure, the details of construction of a typical high-quality 26-footer by Harold Seaman are outlined. There were many variations in selection of material, dimensions, detail, and workmanship from builder to builder.

The stem, deadwood, and stern post are of white oak, cut from 4-inch clear stock. After being cut to profile, the stem is rabbeted to receive the ends of the strakes. The deadwood, used in commercial models, was a massive knee which prevented movement between the lower end of the stem and the forward end of the plank keel. It also insured against separation of the garboards from the plank keel at this point. When the knee was omitted, the stem was bolted directly to the bottom plank. The transom is built of cedar planks with lapped seams. The horizontal segments of the lap are at right angles but the vertical part was slightly oblique, being about 105 degrees from the horizontal. When fastened, it tended to force the surfaces together, ensuring tightness. The obliquity also diminished the likelihood of splitting along the line of rivets. The square 3-inch stern post is tapered from below upwards, 1 inch to the foot. It is mortised into the forward surface of the transom $\frac{1}{2}$ inch. The lower end of the stern post is fastened to the after end of the plank keel, usually by a knee.

The stem, keel, stern post, and transom are erected and permanently fastened together, on top of a platform or building table two or three feet above the floor of the boat shop. The upper part of stem and transom were temporarily fastened to the overhead beams of the shop. A set of molds, representing the desired hull cross section at various points, is temporarily erected upon the plank keel, and fastened to the overhead beams of the shop, as were stem and transom. In some later designs, precut plywood bulkheads were used as molds, and were incorporated permanently into the hull structure. This produced a rigid hull, which was not always an advantage. Some builders used as few as one or two molds for a 26-foot hull while others used five or six, depending on the complexity of the hull contour. These forms determined the cross-section shape of the hull while the previously erected stem, keel, and transom determined its profile.

A builder who had developed a satisfactory set of molds for a hull of given length often employed them unchanged for hulls varying 10 to 20 percent in length. This was a widely accepted and successful practice, a proportionally longer hull frequently being as fast as a shorter hull on the same molds, with the same power. Rarely, a mold was omitted with disastrous results. It was particularly likely when a longer hull was shortened by substituting an aftermold for the contour of the transom.

The plank keel, or bottom plank, was made of 2-inch spruce, sometimes white cedar, or slightly thinner yellow pine. In the 26-footer, it was 24 inches wide so that it required two or three planks which were fastened by splines $\frac{3}{4}$ by 2 inches in size. The curved outer edges of the keel plank were both beveled and rabbeted to receive the garboards. In later hulls the rabbeting was omitted, replaced by a sole plank when the lower edge of the garboards had been planed level with the bottom of the keel. This procedure was not employed by Seaman, being considered inferior.

After keel, stem, transom, and molds were erected, planking was begun. The strakes were applied from below upwards. The garboard was carefully fitted into the keel plank rabbet, stem rabbet, and to the stern post or transom. The upper edge of the plank was beveled at about 45 degrees in its central part to receive the next plank, while the forward quarter, or less, was progressively relieved to form a ship lap. This allowed all planking to be smooth at the stem. Sometimes the same lap was used aft so that the planking was smooth where it lapped the edges of the transom. Usually, the transom edge was cut in multiple flat facets to match the plank ends. A lap gauge and protractor were not used, the builder depending upon experience and eye. Battens and straight edge were used occasionally. As each strake was applied, it was screwed to stem and transom, and riveted to the next strake. Steaming of the strakes was often employed. Strakes were butted between frames and backed by a block. The butts are always well staggered, no more than one within 18 inches of the two frames on each side of any butt. Compression of the butted plank ends was obtained by slightly sloping the saw cuts, the butt block fastenings wedged the ends together. Few early builders scarved plank ends.

The technique of riveting received close attention among the good builders. A hole was drilled across the lap. In this hull, rivets $\frac{1}{8}$ inch in diameter were used with a flat head $\frac{1}{2}$ inch in diameter. The hole was drilled $\frac{1}{64}$ inch smaller and the rivet gently tapped in. The burr or washer, the same size as the head, was pushed over the end of the rivet with a hollow punch. The rivet was clipped $\frac{1}{8}$ to $\frac{1}{16}$ inch beyond the burr and the end peened with a light machinist's hammer. First the cut end of the rivet was flattened, then further light blows made the burr concave and level with the surrounding surface of the soft planking. Considerable tension was exerted by this method in skilled hands. Further, when softer wood was riveted to a harder piece, for instance, cedar planking to oak rib, the rivet in the softer wood tended to curve, giving additional purchase and resistance to motion. During the upsetting and riveting procedure, a helper held a 2-pound flathead hammer against the outside of the rivet as an anvil. The planking was continued, each strake being riveted to its mate in turn at 4-inch intervals. The width and overlap of each strake was carefully checked by girth measurements at each station. Both sides were planked simultaneously. The distance from rivet hole to plank edge was varied slightly in an irregular way to decrease the chance of splitting. Clinch nailing, without burrs, was sometimes used but was not satisfactory.

The planking of hulls with rolled or box garboards deserves special notice. Normally the only strakes which are named are the garboard, next to the keel, and the sheer strake at the top of the sides. The plank next to the garboard is called the tuck strake, or simply tuck. In the after third of hulls of rolled garboard pattern, there is a reverse chine between tuck and garboard, resulting in a planked-up skeg. In large hulls of rolled garboard pattern such as pound boats, the tuck may be the third or fourth plank from the keel. The planks between garboard and tuck are the second or third garboards, or garboard fillers. The tuck is always the upper plank at the reverse chine. In hulls of box garboard pattern, the narrow triangular vertical sides are called the box sides or box fillets. These are between the bottom plank and garboard, the garboard also being the tuck in this design.

The box and rolled garboard were supported internally by short floors extending below the steamed frames, called codwads. These were of ¾- to 1-inch cedar or pine, riveted to the sides of the frames.

After the planking was completed from garboards to sheer, framing was started. The ribs are of clear white oak 1 by 1¼ inch. These were placed in a steam box until flexible. They were then inserted into the hull while hot. Gloves were worn and a short length of 2-inch pipe was used over the ends for purposes of manipulation. The frames were bent on the flat, on 8-inch centers. They were held in position with clamps until cool. The frames were drilled and riveted to each strake at the lap of the seams, and to the plank keel. Frames were one piece from sheer to sheer. Occasionally, and particularly in large hulls, frames were sprung in from one side of the plank keel to the opposite sheer, to conserve long material. At the forward end it was not possible to bend a single frame of oak to the sharp bottom contour. These partial frames, or cripples, were butted against the bottom plank. Sometimes a short floor timber was riveted to the sides of the lower ends of the cripples, and to the bottom. The forward and aft frames were sloped toward the ends slightly. The last frames at the ends were omitted. Because of the close quarters, burrs were outside. Some builders reversed this, used screws, or even clinch nails. Filler blocks were inserted between the frames, close to the stem and transom, at the sheer, for varying distances. These filled the voids between planking and clamp. A one piece clamp of oak, from $1\frac{1}{4}$ by $2\frac{1}{4}$ to as large as $1\frac{3}{4}$ by 3 inches, was inserted from stem to transom along the inside of the frames at the sheer. This was cut $\frac{1}{4}$ to $\frac{1}{2}$ inch longer than the measured distance so that it was under compression when sprung into place. A rub strake of white oak was applied along the corresponding outer side of the sheer line. The clamp, frames, and rub strake or rail were drilled and riveted. The rub strake or rub rail was from $1\frac{1}{4}$ by 2 to as large as $1\frac{1}{4}$ by 3 inches. In later boats, some builders decreased the dimensions of the clamp and increased the size of the rub rail. Occasionally, the clamp was omitted, a common practice in the South Jersey beach skiffs.

The sheer was completed by cutting off the projecting ribs flush. In later power boats, a cap or covering piece was applied. A horizontal knee or breast hook was secured by bolts or rivets forward, and corresponding quarter knees at the junction of sheer and transom. Thwart risers were screwed or riveted to the inside of the frames. These were of 3-by-$\frac{7}{8}$-inch cedar or yellow pine.

In the overhanging stern hulls, the lower end of the transom center post was bolted to a longitudinal horn timber of 3-by-$3\frac{1}{2}$-inch white oak. A knee was used to reinforce this junction, and was occasionally mortised. The forward end of the horn timber was bolted through the stern post at the aft end of the garboards. The stern post was drilled for the stuffing box, at right angles to and between the horn timber bolts.

The completed hull of Mr. Seaman's 26-footer weighed 1,200 pounds without engine. Commercial models weighed as much as 200 to 250 pounds more due to heavier scantlings. The engine was mounted on longitudinal, 8-by-2-inch white oak stringers, 12 feet in length. In commercial models they were 16 feet long. The stringers were cut to fit over the top of the frames but were not notched. They were through bolted at 8- to 12-inch intervals. Bulkheads of 3/4-inch pine were secured to frames forward and behind the engine, forming the engine box which held fuel tanks and compartments for odd gear as well. Thwarts were fastened to the risers, with a thwart knee up to the clamp where it was notched. Floors of 3/4-inch cedar or pine were secured to the sides of the frames at intervals of a foot where the hull was wide, increasing to 1 1/2 or 2 foot where the hull narrowed down. The floors added nothing to hull strength, but were merely to support removable floorboards of 5/8-inch pine. In some hulls, the cockpit floor aft of the engine compartment was made water-tight and self-bailing.

For a 22-foot skiff, dimensions were as follows: bottom, 1 3/4-inch spruce or cedar; planking, 5/8-inch white cedar; frames, 3/4-by-1 3/8-inch white oak; stern post 2 7/8-inch square white oak; transom, 1 1/4-inch white cedar; stem, 2 1/4-by-4 1/2-inch white oak; clamp, 5/8-by-1 3/4-inch white oak; risers, 2 1/2-by-5/8-inch cedar; rail caps, 7/8-by-2 7/8-inch white oak; rub strake, 1 1/2-by-7/8-inch white oak. In later years, clear, sound Philippine mahogany, yellow pine, or sometimes white pine was substituted for any wood except the white cedar for planking or white oak for frames. Mahogany was used for planking, on a very selective basis. Number 9 copper nails, 1/2-inch copper burrs, were used for all plank fastening. Brass or bronze screws were used at stem and transom.

In a 16-foot general service skiff, dimensions were as follows: bottom 1 5/8 inch, planking 1/2 or 5/8 inch, frames 1 1/8 by 5/8, transom 1 1/8 inch, stern post 2 3/4-inch square, stem 1 7/8-by-4-inch stress-bent white oak, clamps 1 3/8 by 5/8, rub strakes 1 1/4 by 7/8, and risers 2 by 1/2 inch. The wood used was the same as in the 22-footer with the exception of the stem. Stress bending was not successful in larger sizes. Fastenings were the same.

The completed 22-foot hull weighed 600 pounds and the 16-foot hull 400 pounds without engine, shaft and tanks. The 22-footer was sometimes built to somewhat heavier scantlings for commercial use. The 16-footer was sometimes built to slightly lighter scantlings for tender or sports use.

Mr. Seaman was particularly attentive to selection of materials for his pound boats. Each timber and plank was examined, turned and examined again, before final milling. It was examined again after milling and before incorporation into the hull. Standards of construction and fit were to his usual high standards. In a standard 32-footer, the bottom was 4-inch spruce or yellow pine, fastened together with 1½-by-3-inch splines of the same. The vertical keelson was 3½-by-10-inch spruce or yellow pine. Planking, parting boards, and incidental members were of ⅞-inch white cedar. Some earlier hulls had been planked with full length strakes, dimensions unobtainable after World War I. The stern was of 3¼-by-5½-inch white oak. The transom was 2-inch spruce. The stern post was 3½-inch white oak. Knees, breast hooks were of 2-inch hackmatack or oak crooks. The thwarts were 3-by-12-inch cedar. The frames were 1½-by-2½-in. white oak. The risers were 4-by-⅞-inch white cedar. The clamps were 3-by-⅞-in. and rub strakes 2½-by-1¼-inch white oak. Planking was riveted with number 8 copper nails and ¾- or ⅞-inch burrs at 2-inch intervals. The planking was fastened to the frames with ¼-inch Swedish iron, oval head rivets. This unusual fastening was needed because of the great load of fish and water when beached. The hulls leaked when hauled with a load, but not when the hull was supported by the sea. After being unloaded, the elasticity of frames and planking closed the leaks promptly. A finished 32-foot pound boat weighed 3½ tons without engine, shaft, and tanks.

White or red oak sheathing of 1½ to 2 inches was applied to the bottom as protection when beaching. Strips of 1-by-2-inch white oak were fastened to the strakes at their laps, except for 4 feet at bow and stern, to protect against chafing of the sides on pound poles. Additional rub strakes, and occasionally half-round iron, were applied at the sheer.

Builders were generally careful in selecting material. Cedar was sometimes mined in south or central New Jersey swamps, where windfallen trees were preserved under water almost indefinitely. Much eastern white cedar was cut locally, was available in lengths to 30 feet, and was always bought flich sawn. Another type, pinhole cedar, contained many very small knots, was of the same genus, and was very resistant to splitting. Local cedar sold for 7¢ a foot in the mid-1930's. By 1940, most cedar was cut in the Carolinas, and was increasingly difficult to obtain in lengths. Philippine mahogany, and occasionally marine plywood sawed into planks, are increasingly used in place of cedar. The uniform strength of plywood is disliked and distrusted by the older and better builders. Long-leaf yellow pine has proved excellent for bottom planks but its occasional use for hull planking has been only experimental, and disappointing. The only usable material for frames and clamps is clear white oak. Other varieties are not used.

Knees, breast hooks, and quarter hooks are sawn from oak crotches or hackmatack. Apple, cedar, and sassafras were formerly used. Many early builders cruised local woods in upper Ocean County, Freehold, Howell, Wall, Atlantic, and Holmdel Townships for timber. Local mills in the same areas, notably Flitcroft's, Applegate's, Heyer's, Brocklebank's, and Reid's, supplied the local timber. The last, J. R. Reid's mill in East Freehold, was in operation to 1966. In late years, Reid supplied locust posts for horse racing rather than boat material. Oak knees were obtained by blasting out stumps from swamps, then dressing into flat stock. Formerly, all timber was air dried for a year, then for a second year by the boat builder, out of the weather.

In recent years, higher power and greater speed have imposed changes in traditional construction. Mahogany, by virtue of greater hardness, is more resistant about fastenings. The triangular gap between the frame and strake left a segment of planking unsupported. In the bottom planking, these voids are commonly filled with wood wedges or knuckles. The increasing flare and clipper stem profile of some modern hulls impose unusual contours on the planks. Some are subjected to real torture. Some builders shape a strake in several sections which are scarved and glued, before application to the hull. Plywood is used in the same way. In some modern skiffs, the bottom planking is white cedar with knuckles between frame and plank, the curve of the bilge is planked with mahogany, and the sheer portion of the sides with plywood which is of complex shape and bears the lights or ports.

A relatively recent addition has been the use of a hogging clamp or stringer to add longitudinal strength without undesirable rigidity. This is of oak and extends from lower stem to lower transom, and well above the turn of the bilge amidships. It is fastened to the inner aspect of all the frames it crosses. A few builders use a plank keelson, nearly the length of the keel. This is laid in place, marked at each frame, removed, carefully mortised for each frame, reinserted, then fastened. In the hands of a craftsman, this adds greatly to strength with little weight. Higher speeds, increased power, greater beam may require even additional internal reinforcement.

Luting was not used by early builders except about a well. All joints were wood-to-wood and were sharp tool finished, not sanded. Some builders avoided power drills because the wood was scorched by friction. Modern reliable nonhardening seam compounds are increasingly employed. Their use has made boat builders out of many house carpenters. In the hands of a skilled builder, their use affords more continued resistance to leaking under conditions of unusual stress, or when going overboard in the spring.

A few oddities have been noted while examining boats and construction. A number of hulls prove to have unequal half girths. The inequality has been as much as 4 inches in a 30-foot hull. No estimate of performance or handling characteristics was obtainable. In two skiffs, the number of strakes was asymmetrical. In one, the half girths were the same, but in the other, the builder seemingly omitted a plank on one side. One hull was examined which was of sheet iron or steel. This had the contour of a lap-strake skiff hull, complete with longitudinal corrugations corresponding to planks. It appeared never to have been completed. In the fiberglass era, molded sea skiff-type hulls have been built, using successful lap-strake hulls as mold or model. The Z-shaped longitudinal corrugations add rigidity to the thin skin. Exaggerated bottom corrugations may aid in high speed hulls as longitudinal steps.

There were some regional differences in construction of skiffs of similar or nearly identical model. In central and lower Ocean County, separated from Monmouth in 1850, narrower and more numerous strakes were used. In a 17- or 18-foot hull, Monmouth builders employed 7 or 8 strakes while Ocean builders used 10 or 11. The planking in Ocean County tended to be slightly thicker, particularly in pound boats. It is not possible to discriminate further as individual differences between builders could be quite marked.

Today there are few men with the experience, training, skill and self-discipline needed to construct a sea skiff to the old standards.

SOURCES

All the data were obtained by observation and interview with the following builders. In a few cases, published catalogs and builders' specification records were available.

Carl Adams, Smithville
Joseph E. Banfield, Ocean Township
Donald M. Campbell, Belmar
Robert D. Campbell, Belmar
Capt. John Kocsik, Spring Lake Heights
Henry Luhrs, Morgan
John Luhrs, Red Bank
Harold A. Seaman, Port-au-Peck
Harry Van Sant, Atlantic City

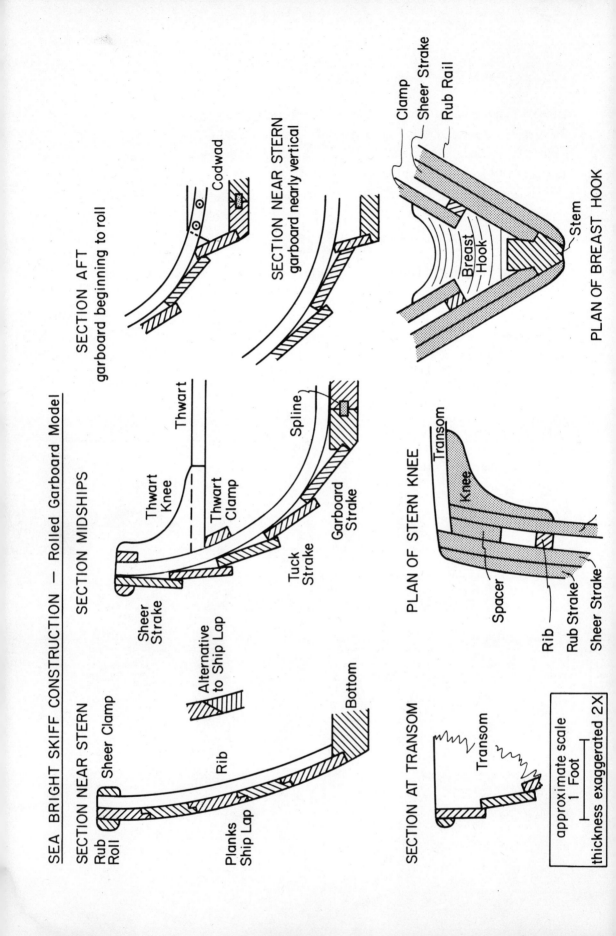

SEA BRIGHT SKIFF CONSTRUCTION — Rolled Garboard Model

SECTION NEAR STERN

SECTION MIDSHIPS

SECTION AFT
garboard beginning to roll

Codwad

SECTION NEAR STERN
garboard nearly vertical

Clamp

Sheer Strake

Rub Rail

Breast Hook

Stem

PLAN OF BREAST HOOK

Thwart

Thwart Knee

Thwart Clamp

Spline

Sheer Strake

Tuck Strake

Garboard Strake

Alternative to Ship Lap

Sheer Clamp

Rub Roll

Rib

Planks Ship Lap

Bottom

PLAN OF STERN KNEE

Transom

Knee

Spacer

Rib

Rub Strake

Sheer Strake

SECTION AT TRANSOM

Transom

approximate scale
1 Foot
thickness exaggerated 2X

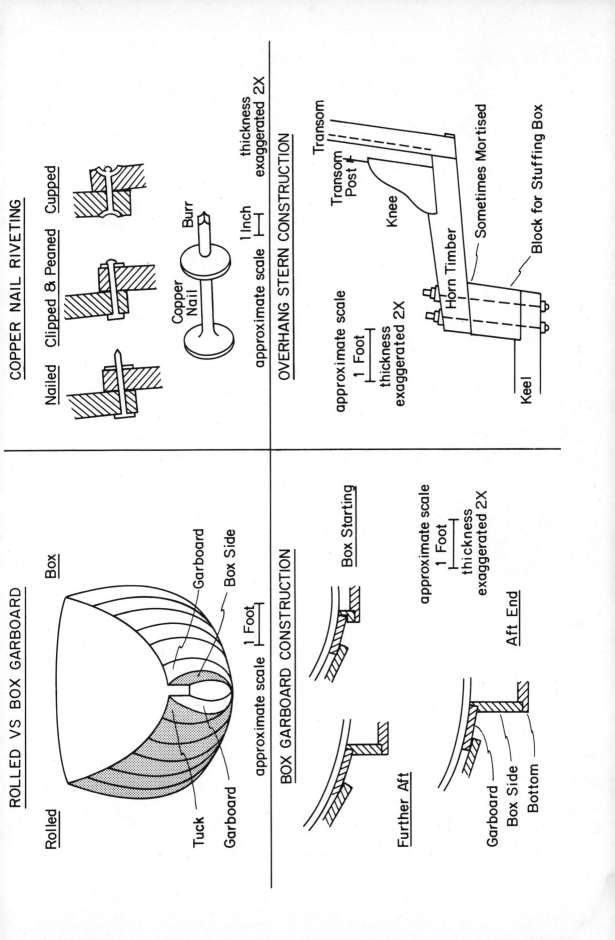

COPPER NAIL RIVETING

Nailed Clipped & Peaned Cupped

Copper Nail
Burr

1 Inch
approximate scale

thickness
exaggerated 2X

OVERHANG STERN CONSTRUCTION

Transom

Transom Post

Knee

Horn Timber

Sometimes Mortised

Block for Stuffing Box

Keel

approximate scale
1 Foot
thickness
exaggerated 2X

ROLLED VS BOX GARBOARD

Rolled

Box

Garboard

Box Side

Tuck

Garboard

1 Foot
approximate scale

BOX GARBOARD CONSTRUCTION

Box Starting

Further Aft

approximate scale
1 Foot
thickness
exaggerated 2X

Aft End

Garboard
Box Side
Bottom

RUDDERS AND STERNS

approximate scale

1 Foot
⊢—⊣

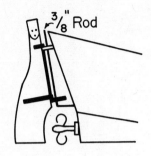

GUDGEONS AND ROD

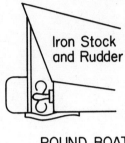

Iron Stock
and Rudder

POUND BOAT

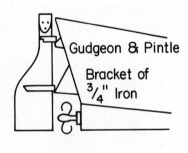

Gudgeon & Pintle

Bracket of
$\frac{3}{4}$" Iron

POUND BOAT

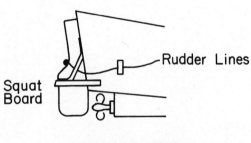

Rudder Lines

Squat
Board

OVERHANG STERN
OUTBOARD RUDDER

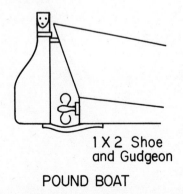

1 X 2 Shoe
and Gudgeon

POUND BOAT

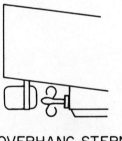

OVERHANG STERN
SPADE RUDDER

– Specifications

17' Bottom "SEA BRIGHT DORIES" Drafts #111A & 111-B.
L.O.A.-#111-A 21' #111-B-20'9" BEAM- 6'6" LEAST DEPTH-32" Other dimensions see draft.

<u>Stem</u>:- Steam-bent white-oak sided 2" moulded as plan. Fastened to bottom with six 5/16" gal. rivets.

<u>Stern-post</u> Draft #111-B:- White-oak sided 3 1/4" moulded as plan. Fastened to bottom with four 5/16" gal. drive bolts and thru skeg with four 5/16" gal. drive bolts.

<u>Shaft-log, trail-timber and stern-post</u> Draft #111-A:- White-oak sided 3 1/4" moulded as plan. Shaft-log reinforced by two one-inch floors or bulk-heads across boat, each floor securely fastened to stern-post, timber and thru plank-laps. Shaft log fastened thru bottom with four 5/16" gal. drive bolts and thru skeg with four 5/16" gal. drive bolts. Trail-timber mortised into shaft-log & fastened with two 5/16" drive-bolts in log and two into floor off side of log. Each foot of the knee at the intersection of the trail-timber and stern-post fastened with four 5/16" gal. rivets.

<u>Stern</u>:- 1 7/8" spruce with 1 1/8" oak top board and 5/16" feather in seams. Stern securely riveted to stern-post.

<u>Bottom</u>:- 17" long, 32" wide by 1 3/4" thick with 1 1/2" feather in seams and rabbited to receive garboard-streaks.

<u>Skeg</u>:- White-oak securely riveted thru bottom and fastened to shaft-log with four 5/16" gal. drive-bolts.

<u>Planking</u>:- Lap-streaks (8 streaks to side) All laps, butts and ends properly fit and set in white-lead. Plank-fastening #9 round copper rivits thru laps spaced at, 3" c's and #10 brass screws where impossible to thru fasten. All fastening up stem and stern #10 brass screws. All butts cut between timbers with butt-blocks from timber to timber and securely riveted.

<u>Timbers</u>:- White-oak 3/4" X 1 3/8" steam-bent in one piece from gunwhale to gunwhale with cod-wads under at intersection of bottom and garboard-streaks. All timbers thru-fastened thru bottom and plank-laps with #8 round copper riveted over burrs. Timber-heads, gunwhales, planking and clamps thru fastened with #8 copper rivits.

<u>Breast-hook</u>:- White-oak 1 3/8" thick moulded as draft and thru-fastened with 3/16" gal. rivits.

<u>Stern-knees</u>:- 1 3/8" thick hack-me-tack knees as plan. thru-fastened with #8 copper rivits.

<u>Gunwales</u>:- 1" X 1 1/2" white-oak in one piece full length. Fastened as above.

<u>Clamps</u>:- 5/8" X 1 3/8" white-oak in one piece full length. Fastened as above.

<u>Caps</u>:- 7/8" X 3" white-oak, steam-bent, one piece full length. Fastened to gunwhales and clamps with 1 1/2" boat nails a 6" c's.

<u>Row-locks</u>:- Thole-pins with 7/8" holes in caps as plan.

<u>Risers</u>:- 5/8" X 3" cedar 10 1/2 inches down from caps as plan.

<u>Rowing-seats</u>:- 1 1/8" X 10 spruce. Forward seat loose and second and third seats kneed in with hackmetack knees as plan. Knees securely fastened to edges of seats and thru-fastened thru laps and heads, same as timbers.

<u>Pen-boards</u>:- 5/8" cedar under second and third seats and securely fastened to timbers.

<u>Center-board Trunk</u>:- kneed in and fastened to forward pen-board as plan.

<u>Motor-space</u>:- Bulkheads and top 5/8" cedar.

<u>Stern-locker</u>:- 5/8" cedar. Bearers of 7/8" X 4" spruce as plan.

<u>Motor-Beds</u>:- White-oak as plan. Thru-fastened with 3/8" gal. rivits.

<u>Rudder</u>:- Spruce with white-oak tiller and hung as plan.

Boat primed, plugged, puttied and painted 2nd coat.

THE SEA BRIGHT DORY WORKS.
Long Branch, N.J.

Specifications made about 1920 for a 21-foot Sea Bright dory on a U.S. Government contract. Seaman Boat Works (the Sea Bright Dory Works).

Keel and skeg assemblies.

Steamed strakes applied and clamped in place.

Modern skiff construction at the Ulrichsen Works. The first four strakes have been applied.

Planking nearly completed. Ulrichsen Works.

Interior of a planked and framed Ulrichsen skiff.

Engine installation.

Preassembled trunk cabin and deck house.

Transom planking completed.

Completed Ulrichsen skiffs.

Sheet-iron sea skiffs.

5

The Rum Runners

Shortly after the Prohibition Amendment went into effect in 1920, Rum Row was established off the entrance to New York Harbor. The great rewards of landing a cargo of illicit beverages attracted a number of local boatmen. They put out from local harbors, purchased a cargo on the Row, and returned to reap their gains. Initially, any and all types of boats that could go to sea three miles were used. The Sea Bright skiff was commonly employed.

Countermeasures by law enforcement agencies made speed necessary, almost from the start. This was added easily to the already seaworthy skiff. In the early 1920's, open 28-footers powered by 60 H.P. Pierce Arrow engines, making 15 M.P.H. empty, were used. They came to the Row with one man steering and one man pumping, always full speed ahead.

The Kofoed Boat Works of Keyport had a reputation for fast, seaworthy, sturdy skiffs. In the early 1920's they built a pair of conventional 42-foot skiffs powered by single 190 H.P. Mianus engines. They had a speed of 22 knots when loaded to their capacity of 400 to 500 cases of liquor. Their success prompted construction of two more of the same model, lengthened to 46 feet, but with the same power. The new skiffs had a carrying capacity of 1,000 cases, with speed only slightly diminished.

Both rum runner and Coast Guard were competing for the construction of faster boats, often in the same boat shop. It was not unusual to see an obvious rum runner under construction while next to it a Coast Guard cutter was being built. Both may be of similar size and model and each side had free access to the secrets of the other. The builders of the rum runner were able to make immediate, and last-minute, alterations in design and detail, an advantage not available to the Coast Guard. A rum runner could have a last-minute reduction of fuel capacity, reduction of freeboard, another engine added, or trunk cabin replaced by decking.

The end of World War I left a large number of unused, powerful aircraft engines as surplus. This was a windfall for the rum runners, as they were vastly more powerful, cheaper, and lighter than any marine engine. They were first used with little conversion beyond a coupling for attachment to a marine clutch. Later, special kits, and parts for marine conversion were produced. One of the most popular conversions locally was produced by the Vimalert Company of Jersey City, the 450 H.P. Vimalert-Liberty becoming standard among many Monmouth County builders.

The Liberties were used in smaller skiffs at first. Banfield of Leonardo produced a small number of successful boats using their 28-, 32- and 38-foot standard hulls powered by single engines. Charles Cliamont in the Keyport area built several skiffs about 30 feet long, powered by direct connected, unconverted single Liberties. They were fast but inconvenient to maneuver. Many other builders, King of Highlands, Hankins of Lavalette, Proal of Red Bank, and Seaman of Long Branch built Liberty-powered boats from 28 to 32 feet in length. By this time, newer conversions by Sellick and Capitol were making the somewhat finicky Liberty more reliable.

Three very successful Coast Guard chasers were built by E. Fell Jardine of Atlantic City in 1925, of conventional Sea Bright skiff design. These 40-footers, CG-2244, 2245, and 2246, were of relatively low profile and less burden than rum runners of the same size. They were powered by a pair of Gar Wood Liberties and made 42.5 M.P.H. on trials.

An increase in the speed of Coast Guard vessels caused the introduction of somewhat larger multiengined rum runners. An example was the "Wee" built by Kofoed. This was 50 feet by 14 feet and drew $3\frac{1}{2}$ feet unloaded. The planking was 1-inch cedar and the 4-foot wide bottom plank was of 3-inch yellow pine. She was of conventional Sea Bright skiff construction, modified by a straighter sheer, flat run and broad flat-bottomed transom. The box garboard design was continued and power was furnished by a pair of 400 H.P. Liberties.

The "Wee" was an immediate success. The 400 H.P. conversions were replaced with a pair of more powerful conversions. Later, a third engine was installed, giving greater speed and requiring little more room. Two sister ships, the "Fleur-de-lis" and the "Lily of the Valley" were built, with minor modifications. Their service speed was 25 to 35 miles per hour with a load of 500 cases.

The Proal Works introduced hulls with smooth planked bottoms, and conventional lap strake above the turn of the bilge. The smooth planking was ship lap, although standard caravel planking with heavier strakes, was used later. Proal built boats with two, three and four engines.

The Liberty was not the only large engine in use. By the 1930's, the Wright Cyclone and the Sterling Viking were used increasingly. The Viking, a 565 H.P., 8-cylinder engine with 8-inch bore and 9-inch stroke, earned a reputation for requiring rare service and few overhauls. In contrast, the Liberty souped up to produce 500 H.P. was in need of constant tuning and much repair. Some later rum runners used combinations of engines, for instance a Wright Cyclone was used for ordinary cruising, flanked by a pair of Vikings to be used at high speed.

A number of the lightly built rum boats developed serious longitudinal weakness. This resulted in shaft and bearing failures, as well as loss of watertight integrity. Application of external hogging strakes at the sheer, and internal stringers were used. In at least one boat, stringers were passed through holes cut in the transom. Other boats later required reinforcing transversely by the installation of sawn frames in segments. The Kofoed boats were exceptionally strong, one being in use as a party boat in 1964, although much modified.

The Sea Bright skiff rum boats were progressively, but never completely, replaced by boats of V-bottom design. Some of these were the work of prominent naval architects while others were scaled up adaptions of runabouts and commuters. They were cheaper to build than the Sea Bright designs, were more tolerant of poorer materials, and did not require the same craftsmanship. The better examples were capable of sustained speed in rough seas, beyond the capabilities of the British-designed American-built World War II P.T. boats.

In the later years of rum running, the limit of offshore Coast Guard patrol was increased from three to twelve miles, and recommissioned World War I destroyers used for patrol. The superior sea-keeping abilities and speed of the destroyers made the size and cost of rum runners much greater, and the chances of success less. However, the builders had learned lessons valuable in later application to pleasure craft.

SOURCES

Publications

Van De Water, Frederick F. *The Real McCoy*. London, 1930.
Willoughby, Malcolm F. *Rum War at Sea*. Washington, 1964.

Anecdotal Material and Photographs

From all the sources noted in the preceding chapters.

Forty-two-foot Kofoed rum runner skiff. Note the lap-strake construction and closely spaced bent oak frames.

The skiff was powered by a 190-H.P. Mianus engine.

Forty-six-foot Sea Bright skiff rum runner. Note the house forward and lap-strake construction.

Fleur-de-Lis in lower Arthur Kill. Note the lap-strake construction and level run at high speed.

Fleur-de-Lis under way.

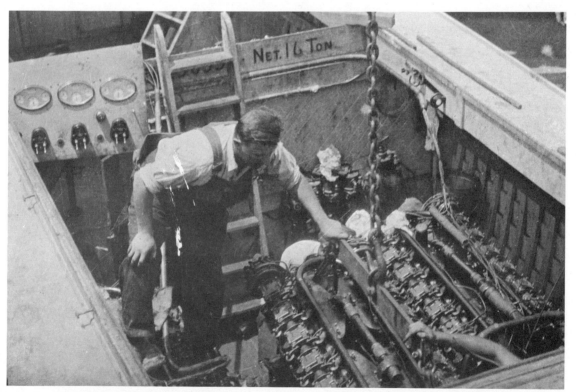

Engine room of the *Fleur-de-Lis* about 1930. A Liberty engine has just been replaced. The engine instruments and switches can be seen on the board secured to the forward engine room bulkhead.

The new engine being lowered into place.

Proal rum runner built in 1931, with V-bottom. Some were built with U sections forward, lap-strake construction above water, as a design compromise.

Rum runner built by Pierre Proal. Proal craft were comparatively high-sided, had more deadrise forward, and were smooth planked from keel to bilge. Later similar models approached a V-bottom.

6

The Surf Boats

The New Jersey and Long Island coasts converge on the entrance to New York Harbor at right angles. In the days of sail, the Jersey beaches, obscured by weather, were a dangerous lee shore during winter gales from the northeast. A vessel unable to work to windward was driven progressively into shoal water, and finally onto the bars offshore. The most reliable navigational aid was the lead line. The veteran coaster kept east of the six-fathom mark, about a mile offshore, and east of the eight-fathom mark, about two miles, in weather. The Long Island coast was rarely a lee shore, but was dangerous when latitude had been miscalculated, a noon sight not possible, or when sea room to avoid the Jersey beaches had been overestimated.

The surf boats were developed for life-saving and wrecking off the New Jersey beaches. Their model was the same as the smaller beach skiffs, developed for fishing. Both were designed for launching through the surf and to survive offshore, were constructed by the same builders, and used by the same surfmen or fishermen, depending upon the needs of the moment.

The first reliable information on the surf boats is in an 1846 New Jersey report by a legislative commission. Three legislators, Peter

Vredenburgh, John S. Darcy, and Jonathan C. Ten Eyck, were appointed by Governor Charles C. Stratton to investigate charges against inhabitants of the coast of Monmouth County, at that time extending from Sandy Hook to Little Egg Harbor Inlet. The charges, refusal to give relief to perishing passengers and crewmen, plundering the dead, and extracting money for the delivery of bodies, arose following the wreck of the ship *John Minturn*. The charges were made by members of the crew to the American Shipwreck Society of New York. They were taken up by the press, particularly in New York, and magnified to include wholesale charges of land piracy and even murder.

The report consists of the sworn (in the case of the Quakers, affirmed) depositions of local inhabitants, the coroner's memorandum book, and correspondence. It disproves the serious charges and indicates the guilt of some of the crew of the *Minturn*. In so doing, it gives much valuable data, including the use of the term "surf-boat."

The shore was divided into districts, each under a wreckmaster. These were local residents of substance and good reputation, frequently retired shipmasters or surfmen, who were responsible for saving wrecked passengers and crew, and for retrieving salvageable cargo. Occasionally an intact stranded vessel could be salvaged as well.

The wreckmasters from Sandy Hook to Green's Pond, the present Lake Takanasee, were Henry Wardell and James Green; from Green's Pond to Manasquan Inlet, John Remson; from Manasquan to the site of the closed Cranberry Inlet, the present Seaside Park, Hugh Johnson; and from Cranberry Inlet to Barnegat Inlet, Joseph Lawrence. Retired wreckmasters were Samuel A. and John S. Forman and Capt. David Newberry. The legislators' report imparts a great aura of respect for the words and judgments of the wreckmasters and surfmen.

The wreckmasters were owners or part owners of surf boats. Each boat had a crew of four oarsmen and a coxswain, and were carried on land on a wagon drawn by a team of horses. At the time of the report, there were about ten surf boats distributed along the shore.

The general impression of the statements of the forty-odd deponents in the report is that of personal hardihood, and the ability to come to terms with the hostile environment and its effects.

The next information is contained in an address to the House of

Representatives by Congressman William A. Newell of New Jersey in 1848. Newell reported that the coast between Sandy Hook and Little Egg Harbor was more famous for shipwrecks than any other part of the country, including the Florida reefs. In a little more than nine years preceding July 31, 1848, 158 vessels had been wrecked on the Jersey coast including ships, brigs, schooners, sloops, and pilot boats; and 180 vessels had been wrecked on the adjacent Long Island coast. These statistics had been gathered by Newell from some of his constituents, some of whom had been deponents in the 1846 legislative commission report. There was no national agency or regular register of shipwrecks or marine disasters.

Newell, a physician, pointed out that the shore was made especially dangerous by a sand bar from 300 to 800 yards offshore, covered by not more than two feet of water. A stranded vessel's crew and passengers are separated from the safety of the shore by an impassable surf, while the vessel is breaking up beneath them. The ordinary ship's longboat is not able to pass over the bar while a surf boat will, and will survive in a sea, and come to shore when the other would be swamped.

The most important portion of the address was an amendment to the Light House Bill for $10,000 to provide surf boats, rockets, carronades, and other necessary apparatus for the better protection of life and property from shipwrecks on the coast of New Jersey, between Sandy Hook and Little Egg Harbor. The amendment was unanimously adopted, and represents the establishment of the Life Saving Service.

The two previous reports indicate that the surf boat was long established, well recognized, and widely used on the Jersey coast, and also that its excellence prompted its inclusion as a necessary part of the apparatus for lifesaving. However, there is no description of it, beyond the name.

The next link is furnished by the Report of the Secretary of the Treasury for 1858. This recounts performance trials of surf boats, viewed by a committee at Sea Bright. Among those tested were Wardell's surf boat and Green's surf boat. Both are described as old, belonging on the beach, behaving handsomely with their skilled and practiced crews. They were very similar, clinker-built of cedar, square stern, no air chambers, rowing six oars. They were 26 feet overall, 22 feet keel, 7 feet beam, 30 inches deep amidships, 20 inches sheer on top, 8 inches sheer on keel, and weigh about 950 pounds.

Another tested in the same trials was Bunker's model surf boat. It was clinker-built of 3/4-inch cedar, copper fastened and riveted, with a square stern 3 feet wide on top. It rowed four oars and had detached air chambers at stem, stern and under the thwarts on each side. It was 24 feet 8 inches long, 20 feet on the bottom, 6 feet in beam, 28 inches deep amidships, 20 inches sheer on top, 9 inches sheer on keel and weighed about 700 pounds. It was described as possessing great buoyancy, lightness and strength. The model made her peculiarly serviceable in the surf and met the existing wants of the life-saving stations.

Another group became interested in the life-saving stations. The Philadelphia Board of Trade published a report in 1860 which gave a brief history of the development of British lifeboats in contrast to the American experience. The Americans had found that light, strong, elastic boats, in our waters, were better than the heavier British design. It indicated that fifty-four boats of the Bunker model had been built in New York and in Toms River, N.J. An unofficial test by four Cape May area boat builders reported the Bunker boats to be of inferior workmanship, and useless as lifeboats. They are also described as square-sterned whaleboat models, no better than those used on the coast forty years before.

The Cape May critics went unheeded, the transom stern, lap-strake surf boats of various models being widely used. An incomplete *Record of Boats of the U.S. Life Saving Service* from 1873 to 1902 records the builders, dimensions, duration of service, and cost of the surf boats. The New Jersey builders were Henry C. Lane of Long Branch, Jacob Herbert of Manasquan, Charles H. Huff of East Long Branch, Forman Hulse of Osbornville and Mantoloking, Lawrence B. Newman of Long Branch and Squan Beach, Michael Allen of Toms River, Samuel G. Gandy of Cape May Court House, and an unnamed builder from Camden. Other builders were J. C. Smith of 404 Water Street in New York City, Stephen Roberts of Harlem, New York, and J. T. Hutson of Baltimore.

The surf boat models were described as "Long Branch," "Squan," "Havens," "Havens and Mayville," and "Mayville." There is no obvious difference among the models in size or specifications so they probably relate to arrangement and equipment. The Squan and Long Branch models were the most common; only a few of the others were recorded. These latter, used in Cape May County stations, were built by Gandy; with the exception of one Havens model by Hulse, which was used at Mantoloking. The dimensions of each boat are recorded and are remarkable for lack of uniformity. No two boats, by the same builder, were quite the same size, regardless of model. All boats fall into three general sizes. The smallest were about 23 feet long by 5½ feet beam, with 4 thwarts. The intermediate were 25 feet long by 6½ to 7 feet beam, with 6 thwarts. The largest were 27 feet long by 7 feet beam, with 6 thwarts. The cost was $160 to $175. All were clinker-built with flat bottoms. Most were of copper fastened cedar planking on oak frames but some were pine planked and a few fastened with galvanized iron. The average life of a surf boat was fifteen years, with considerable variation. The fate of individual boats varied from "condemned," to "sold out," "carried to sea and lost," and "considered worthless, used as kindling." A few boats were transferred from one station to another. One boat was exhibited at the Louisville Exposition of 1883, later serving for thirteen years. Another was exhibited at the London Fisheries Exhibition and was returned damaged. Other builders of transom-stern lifeboats were Jared Wade of Sag Harbor, N.Y., and L. Raymond and D. Blackburn of New York City.

There was continued affirmation of the superiority of the cedar surf boat. The 1876 *Report of the Operations of the United States Life Saving Service* supported the conclusions of the 1872 Commission which favored the cedar surf boat, then in general use by the wreckers on the Jersey coast, with certain modifications. They considered the resulting model to be an unparalleled success by means of which thousands of lives were saved. An 1879 article in *Popular Science Monthly* described the cedar surf boat as 6-oared, from 25 to 27 feet long, 5½ to 6 feet beam, and of varying model. The light weight and draft made it the only boat suitable for service on the beaches and shoal waters of the Atlantic and Gulf coasts. A sketch of a surf boat and its beach carriage is included in the article.

Two plans demonstrate the characteristics of the Jersey cedar surf boats. These were a U-shaped transom sloping about 30 degrees, marked sheer, slightly rockered flat bottom, rounded midsections, lap-strake construction and a reverse chine in the after part of the hull between garboard and second strake.

One is a plan drawn by William A. Seaman of Branchport, dating from about 1870. It is a finely modeled hull 25 feet long and 6 feet 4 inches beam. It is of lap-strake construction on closely spaced bent oak frames, has six thwarts for six rowers and uses thole pins. The other was published in Appleton's *Encyclopedia of Applied Mechanics* in 1880. It is a similar, fine-modeled hull 26 feet 2½ inches by 6 feet 9 inches. It is of lap-strake construction over sawn frames, has six thwarts for six rowers and uses row locks.

The surf boats were carried and housed on light, four-wheeled wagons with large, wide-tired wheels. These could be horse drawn to the wreck site, easily traversing beach and dunes, as well as roads.

Self-bailing, self-righting lifeboats of English design had been introduced in 1876. Other similar double-ended boats were subsequently developed and used. Many proved excellent; but the 1890 Life Saving Service report cites the preference for the older cedar surf boats for short distances and where the number of imperiled people was not large, as they were so quickly responsive to the coxswain's tactics.

The New Jersey surf boat or beach skiff saw use during the Civil War. Newberry Havens collected a crew in Long Branch to man a light and easily handled skiff, constructed by Walter Seaman in 1859. It was used to land soldiers during a naval expedition at New Orleans under General Banks in 1861. Seaman and a number of fishermen from Long Branch, including Samuel H. Hayden, saw service in this, possibly in other similar operations.

The transom stern cedar boats continued in use off the New Jersey beaches after 1900, and probably up to 1910, although none was constructed after 1888. Their excellence and sea kindliness were recollected by veteran surfmen until recent years.

The number of wrecks and loss of life diminished with the replacement of sail by steam and wood by steel. The surf boat had always been augmented by the line gun, breeches buoy, and life car. Later, offshore cutters and inlet based power lifeboats made the numerous life-saving stations unnecesary. The life-saving stations, the beach patrols and the surf boats are memory.

SOURCES

Publications

Report of the Commissioners to Investigate the Charges Concerning the Wrecks on the Monmouth Coast, Communicated to the Assembly March 20, 1846. Trenton, 1846.

Remarks of William A. Newell of New Jersey, *On a Proposition to Devise Means for the Preservation of Life and Property from Wrecks on the New Jersey Coast.* Washington, 1848.

Report of Commissioners Appended to the Report of the Secretary of the Treasury for 1858. Washington, 1858.

Report of a Special Committee of the Philadelphia Board of Trade in Relation to the Life-Saving Stations upon the Coast. Philadelphia, 1860.

Report of the Operations of the United States Life Saving Service. Washington, 1876.

O'Connor, W. D. "The United States Life-Saving Service." Extract from Appleton's *Annual Cyclopedia for 1878,* published in *Popular Science Monthly,* 1879.

Kimball, Sumner I. *Organization and Methods of the United States Life-Saving Service.* Washington, 1890.

Sweetland, Reynolds A., and Joseph Sugarman. *Entertaining a Nation.* Long Branch, 1940.

Unpublished Material

"Records of Boats at Stations, 1873–1902." National Archives.

Personal Reminiscences and Anecdotal Material

Reuben Corlies, Manahawkin
Howard K. Hayden, Long Branch
John L. Lockhead, Newport News
Harold A. Seaman, Port-au-Peck
William D. Wilkinson, New York

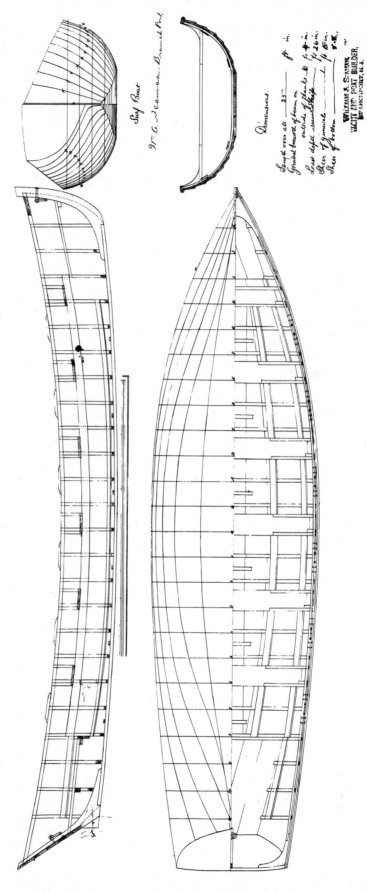

Surf Boat

Wm. A. Seaman, Beaml Port.

Dimensions.

WILLIAM A. SEAMAN,
YACHT AND BOAT BUILDER,
BRANCHPORT, N.J.

The Sea Bright skiff as surf boat, an adaptation for use by the Life Saving Service. This drawing was made by William A. Seaman about 1880. A propeller and engine were pencilled in later. *Courtesy of Harold A. Seaman.*

Life Saving Station Number 5 at Lake Takanesee, formerly Green's Pond, about 1880. The Station was long associated with the Captains Green, who served at wreckmasters, formed volunteer crews, and were captains of later life-saving crews. The surf boat *Ella Green* was probably built by Seaman, and is nearly identical with that shown in the plan. In the foreground is a life car, invented by Captain Douglas Ottinger of the Revenue Service in 1849, and later claimed by Joseph Francis. It was used in place of the breeches buoy in high surf. Also shown is the Lyle gun, projectiles, storm lamp, line sulky, and gun and equipment sulky. The captain and six oarsmen in the foreground wear cork-buoyed life jackets. Two reserves are on lookout and another stands at the far side of the lifeboat. *Courtesy of Howard K. Hayden.*

A line engraving of Life Saving Station Number 5, obviously copied with background changes, from the photograph. It appeared in *Harper's New Monthly Magazine*, February, 1882.

Surf boat at Life Saving Station Number 4, Monmouth Beach. From *Illustrated Christian Weekly,* April 28, 1887. *Courtesy of William D. Wilkinson.*

"The New Surf-Boat and Boat Wagon," from *Frank Leslie's Illustrated Newspaper,* April 11, 1874. *Courtesy of William D. Wilkinson.*

Surf boat and boat wagon, about 1885. The Navesink Highlands in the background. *Courtesy of the Mariners Museum.*

Surf boat from Bay Head Life Saving Station being rolled up the beach, about 1885. *Courtesy of Axel B. Carlson.*

Life Saving Station Number 4. From *Album of Long Branch*, J. H. Schenck, 1868. *Courtesy of Daniel Hennessey.*

U. S. Life-saving Station No. 4,

At Long Branch.

MANY years since, these stations for marine relief were established by Government, upon the entire coast, at intervals of ten miles. Ten years since, their number was increased two fold, being now found every five miles.

As a matter of general interest, we give a view of the station at Long Branch, the officer in charge looking seaward and a portion of the crew as if preparing for action. An idea of the practical working will form the best description: Upon the discovery of a vessel in distress, signal rockets indicate that relief is at hand and the crew are summoned to the rescue. A 24 lb. shot from a mortar, carries a line over the vessel, with which communication is at once established, and written directions are sent in a bottle for the management of the life car. This is a shell of galvanized sheet iron, somewhat of an egg form, in which five or six persons may be stowed safely, with percolations for the admission of air in the upper half. This car at least, has never failed to land safely all who have ventured in it. A large open life boat is mounted upon wheels in constant readiness to be moved to any point where numbers are to be landed through the surf. The first vessel relieved at this point, was the ship Adonis. Her crew of eighteen were taken off in March, 1859, for which the N. Y. Life-saving Association presented the station officer, Mr. Chas. H. Green, a splended gold medal. During the first five months of the year 1867, five vessels were relieved.

For these important services, rendered gratuitously to vessels, involving fearful exposure in the heaviest storms, the Government allows the pittance of $200 a year! It is cause for regret, that the system is not placed upon a basis befitting so humane a purpose and removed beyond the reach of political influence.

Description of Life Saving Station Number 4. From *Album of Long Branch. Courtesy of Daniel Hennessey.*

Life Saving Station Number 6 at the lower end of Deal Lake, about 1885. *Courtesy of the Mariners Museum.*

Life Saving Station Number 3 at Sea Bright, about 1885. *Courtesy of the Mariners Museum.*

Interior of a Life Saving Station. From *Harper's Young People,* January 25, 1881. *Courtesy of William D. Wilkinson.*

(*Opposite page.*) The operation of surf boats was a joint enterprise. An "Article of agreement of a Surf Boat," dated April 13, 1835, is preserved among the Forman papers in the Monmouth County Historical Association. The owners, John S. Forman, Morris Freeman, and William Akins agreed to build and own a large sea boat for the purpose of working at wrecks. The document notes that in addition to sharing the ownership, they are "to agree in the selecting of the man to go in the stern of said boat or be captain." Forman was a Manasquan lawyer and Freeman a boat builder. Akins was a retired shipmaster and surfman. A fourth party to the agreement, John Morris, did not sign the document. *Forman Papers, Courtesy of Monmouth County Historical Society.*

This Article of agreement made this 13th April 1835 by and Between John S Forman Esqr Wm Akins John Morris and Morris Freeman all of the Township of Howell County of Monmouth and State of New Jersey Witnesseth

That they the Said Forman Akins Morris & Freeman do Build and Own a Large Sea boat for the Purpose of working at Wrecks that they are Each one of them to pay an Equal Share of the Expence of Said Boat as long as they own her together further any one of the Said men Should feel Dissatisfied and wish to Sell they are Bound and by these Presents do Bind themselves to Sell to their fellow Partner or Portners in Preferance to any one else Provided they will buy.

They are also to agree in the selecting the man to go in the Stern of Said boat or be Captain if any one of the owners Should be Absent when the Boat is wanted to work or the man whom he puts in his Place be absent the remaining owners Shall fill Such vacency with whome they see fit

also if any one of the owners or the men that they put in their place do not perform to the Satisfaction of the Rest it shall be rite for the rest of the owners to Discharg Such man and Get some one Else untill they are Satisfied

In witness where unto we have Signed our Respective names with our Seals the day and year above Writen

Present
Abraham S. Osborn

William B. Hill

John S Forman

William Akins

Morris Freeman

7

The Pleasure Craft

The pound boat, beach skiff, and surf boat had little appeal to the boating public. However, to a discerning few, there were obvious advantages over the ordinary pleasure craft available. The advantages were seakindliness, safety, and durability, with light weight.

The division between cruising and sports-fishing types occurred early. The future development of the latter type will be outlined separately.

The general requirements of the pre-World War I pleasure boating public were protection from the weather and sanitary facilities. An early example of a Sea Bright skiff with trunk cabin was built in 1913 by Lawrence Newman for a Long Branch summer resident, Arthur Byron, an actor. It was on pound boat lines with somewhat reduced freeboard, 30 feet long and with a beam of 10 feet. At about the same time, a similar boat was built by Harold Seaman for Jacob F. Oberle of Newark. This was on a similar, slightly smaller, model pound boat 24 feet in length with an 8-foot beam. Both had a forward trunk cabin, a small enclosed head, two bunks, and a shelf for an alcohol stove. Later, a wheel was installed on the cabin bulkhead. Both these pioneer efforts were successful, and spurred sporadic local interest. Another example was built by Joseph Banfield in 1917. This trunk cabin skiff, the *Dollie R.*, was 26 feet long, with a beam of 8½ feet. It was still in use in 1966.

Further development came during the boom years following World War I. Local builders provided boats of increasing complexity, beauty and utility. Kofoed of Keyport built two standard hulls, 26 and 36 feet in length. The smaller was supplied completely open, with a small forward house, or with raised forward deck. The larger was a trunk cabin model with windshield and canopy top. The smaller boats were capable of 28 M.P.H. with a 150 H.P. Scripps engine, and the larger 20 M.P.H. with the same power.

One of Kofoed's principal innovations was the development of a 20-foot skiff with a raised forward deck which he called the *Sea Bird*. It was a happy combination of good construction, serviceability and performance. In good condition, it would make 38 M.P.H. with 150 H.P. A large number were built, and served well in the bay, and offshore in good weather. They were later built in modified form by Henry Luhrs, who developed the design further. Similar craft were built by Zobel and many others.

The Banfield Company produced standard design 32- and 34-foot boats with several variations of cabin and windshield arrangement. They were supplied with single or twin engines, but were always constructed with a box garboard. In addition to high quality, Banfield was a pioneer in application of mass production methods. All planks and timbers were precut, rabbeted and planed from patterns. The assembly of the hull from its matched parts was rapid, the longest time being required for the drying of paint and varnish. Because of his superior methods and early financial success, Banfield employed a large number of the previously self-employed local boat builders, providing an unequaled pool of skilled labor. The seaworthiness of his boats was proved by the uncomfortable but successful voyage of a 32-foot skiff from New York to Bermuda in 1928. The handsome and able Banfields dominated the field for a number of years, spreading the reputation and name of the Sea Bright skiff far beyond its home waters. Some

5,000 were sold and widely distributed. Banfield also adapted the same hull design to the runabout field in competition with the then popular Gar Wood and Chris Craft models. The Banfields were superior in seaworthiness, but were introduced at a time when all boat sales were suffering the effects of the depression.

The King boat works at Highlands built standard 22- and 28-foot models, based upon a patented hull design. Both sizes were comparatively very fast with low power. The 22-foot model was capable of 30 M.P.H. with 75 H.P. and the 28-foot model of 25 M.P.H. with 150 H.P. The King patent, granted in 1920, featured a transverse concavity and reverse curve of the after part of the bottom. This prevented settling of the stern at higher speeds, but made for a wet boat.

Pierre Proal of Red Bank produced a number of good cruiser-type skiffs which performed well but were not as attractive in appearance as some other contemporary designs.

Seaman produced a continuing stream of high-grade skiffs which were very well balanced in speed, performance and cruising radius. By comparison, some competing designers produced very fast boats which were seriously hampered in range by high fuel consumption and limited fuel capacity. Seaman exerted much ingenuity in space utilization and produced boats of very pleasing appearance. Another small but important feature were permanently secured foot rungs on the transom, a necessity in getting aboard out of the water. These were occasionally removed by owners, on one occasion with tragic results.

A number of other builders supplied individually a small number of pleasure craft each. They differed very little from the boats already described. One builder, Hans W. Wulf, attempted to adapt one hull size to a variety of uses, with reasonably good results. Other builders of excellent pleasure skiffs prior to World War II included Campbell of Belmar, Pearce of Brielle, Hubert Johnson of Bay Head and Charles Hankins of Lavalette, among many others. There was a gradual increase in size, from a range of 30 to 38 feet to that of 36 to 42 feet, by the Second World War. The boats were usually powered by a pair of engines, were more completely equipped for comfortable living, and many now had a flying bridge atop the canopy for increased visibility, and more deck house space.

Great changes took place following World War II. The numbers of boatmen increased rapidly and new builders appeared to fill the demand. Also, builders previously dedicated to supplying the needs of commercial fishermen entered the pleasure boat field. Among the builders or marks were Bay Head Skiffs of Point Pleasant, J. V. Clayton of Keansburg, Clayton of Toms River, Delaney of Keyport, Eastern of Brielle, Galbraith of Keyport, Kulas of Keyport, Olsen of Keyport, Hans Petersen of Keyport, Sica and Silverton of Toms River, Ulrichsen of Marlboro and Zuback of Morgan, and a number more. The greatest change in the past twenty years has been toward appeal to the boatman's wife by providing additional space and comfort for living, the addition of refrigeration, air conditioning, running hot water, and a change in decor from the Spartan to simulation of the modern home. Boats became proportionally wider and higher, with much more glass. The increased height and windage has diminished the seaworthiness of the skiff, although many are still able, safe, and comfortable offshore. They have lost the feel of the older boats in rough weather but the increased power, greater reliability, and better fuel economy of modern engines is a compensation.

More recent innovations in construction have been the use of planking cut from marine plywood, the use of integral plywood bulkheads and nonhardening seam compound. Some of the lap-strake hulls with plywood planking have been exceptionally good, but exceedingly inconsistent in quality, two seemingly identical mass-produced boats behaving very differently in service. Another approach has been the fabrication of lap-strake form in fiberglass, the longitudinal laps acting like the corrugations in sheet metal, and possibly acting as narrow longitudinal steps.

The construction of the sea skiff has spread far beyond New Jersey. In many cases the term is misused by the manufacturer, for the sake of its solid boating reputation and sales appeal. Conversely, there are other manufacturers of well-designed and well-constructed lap-strake boats who do not employ the term sea skiff, though they would be more legitimately entitled to do so.

SPORTS FISHING

Jersey shore anglers had fished off the beaches with hand line and lead squid, later with rod and knuckle duster reels. Off shore and bay fishing were from anchored boats, or by trolling under sail. The usual objective was bluefish or striped bass. The capture of large tuna in the pound nets, a nuisance to the commercial fishermen, presented another challenging objective.

Salt water game fishing attracted followers in the later years of the nineteenth century in California. In 1898 a 183-pound tuna was caught on rod and reel off Catalina Island, and at about the same time the Avalon Tuna Club was founded. New Jersey anglers made occasional offshore fishing expeditions in power skiffs shortly after the turn of the century. A small power skiff had been built by Seaman for Hardy Busch of Newark shortly after 1900, especially for fishing. In the few years just prior to World War I there was increased interest and activity.

Equipment consisted of large-diameter wood reels without gearing, and primitive brakes, mounted on hickory rods. The lines were of linen and were short-lived. Trolling lures were of lead, or lead and cedar, painted or otherwise finished to resemble smaller fish. The equipment was capable of landing bluefish, stripers, and occasional small tuna. Occasional large fish were hooked, but none landed because of line failures.

An early enterprising New Jersey fisherman was William G. Scheer, who was accompanied by his son Otto. Scheer arranged for commercial fishermen to telegraph the sighting of giant tuna or "horse mackerel." He then proceeded to fish the area with dispatch. Scheer had also been able to obtain somewhat more sophisticated equipment, particularly a reel with larger line capacity, than had his predecessors. Scheer hooked one large tuna which he fought for nine hours, only to lose it. The novelist Zane Grey accompanied Scheer on at least one occasion, but without catching any notable fish. Another pioneer New

Jersey fisherman, Jacob Wertheim, succeeded in landing a 285-pound tuna on rod and reel in 1915.

Fishing waned during the war but interest returned in the early 1920's. Highlands was a center and one of the pioneers was Captain Tommy Gifford, who started about 1926. Gifford's first boat was a 28-foot Jersey skiff, powered by a Pierce Arrow engine. The center of the charter-boat fishing industry began to use Shark River as a base about 1929, and Brielle in 1931, after the Manasquan Inlet was reopened.

The Jersey skiff was commonly employed, and increasingly adapted for sports fishing. Francis Low installed a swivel chair in his 22-footer *Mullet* in 1932. The following year he caught a 705-pound tuna off Ambrose Lightship after a five-hour battle. Low, with his captain Fred Wicht, used a newly developed 9/0 Vom Hofe reel, 24-thread line, and a heavy split bamboo rod. During the same year Francis Geer caught several tuna up to 231 pounds off Manasquan Inlet, but lost several larger fish.

There was increasing local interest in angling. Publicity brought sportsmen to the area to participate in this thrilling sport, such a short distance from the great urban centers. Some excellent and experienced boatmen were ashore, and unemployed, since the repeal of Prohibition. Many were drawn to this new, interesting, legal, and initially lucrative field. With the increasing local and general interest, many colorful characters became identified with the sports-fishing industry, the professionals being by all odds more interesting than the customers.

Among the pioneers in Shark River was Herman Guhl who skippered the *Ace*. Other and later professional skippers centered on the Manasquan River were Charles Piercey of the *White Squall*, Buz Garrison of the *Storm King*, Frank McBride of the *Black Hawk*, Warren Mason of the *South Wind*, and the itinerant "Beef" Hall. The skippers had been attracted from commercial fishing, waterfowl guiding, the merchant marine and others, as well as rum running. Their outstanding personal characteristic was independence, most were excellent boatmen, and knowledgeable in the ways of fish. Many of their colorful characteristics have been portrayed in the "Crunch and Des" stories by Phillip Wylie, published in the *Saturday Evening Post*.

By 1940 the charter fleet at the Manasquan reached 250 boats, and additional ones were based at many points on the Barnegat Bay, and farther south along the coast. There were an additional number of boats which were privately owned, or operated on an occasional charter basis. Organization into clubs and the establishment of contests was inevitable. The first were the Manasquan River and the Brielle Marlin and Tuna Clubs. A tuna tournament was held at Atlantic Highlands in 1938, and in following years at the Belmar Basin, the Atlantic City Basin and Montauk Point. The activities were ended by World War II, although catches had fallen off in the preceding few years.

Following the war, Jersey shore big-game fishing never reached its former size or regained its former aura. Increased urbanization, vast increase in privately owned boats, and the diminution of large fish were the cause. In recent years there have been occasional catches of large fish, and variable success in the pursuit of bluefish and striped bass. There are still many hundreds of enthusiastic fishermen in the area. many owning and sailing their own boats.

THE SPEED SKIFFS

Another avenue of the development of the Sea Bright skiff was the Jersey speed skiff, a natural outgrowth of its inherent speed and light weight.

The pioneer effort was the *P.J.*, built in 1922 by Harold Seaman for P. J. Bowers of Red Bank. It was a 15-foot skiff with box or rolled garboards omitted. This was considered a radical departure, to be tried only on an experimental basis, and in a small boat. Powered by a 4-cylinder 22 H.P. Gray, a speed of 21 M.P.H. was possible. Further, it was an able and seaworthy boat.

Seaman recognized that the flat bottom aft, with a high power-to-weight ratio, would produce high performance. He built further models, experimenting with varying ratios of weight, power, and area of planing surface. Larger, lighter engines became available so that a speed of 26 M.P.H. was possible by 1925 and 38 M.P.H. by 1935. New insight indicated that small alterations in the angle between planing surface and propeller thrust were critical. An easy method of altering this was the introduction by Seaman of replaceable wood wedges about 1939.

Interest in racing the speed skiff was led by Sherman Critchfield and Sammy Crooks of Red Bank, and Danny Ardolino of Long Branch. Later boats incorporated an increase in freeboard, an increase in beam, more deadrise forward, and greater flare forward. The standard arrangement was a central engine compartment dividing the hull into forward and aft cockpits.

In the postwar years, the Jersey skiff developed as a closely controlled class, recognized by the A.P.B.A. in 1947. With the use of slightly modified V-8 stock automobile engines, speeds over 60 M.P.H. were attained. Seaman, the originator of the class, built about thirty of them. Other builders were Ralph Mulford of Sea Bright, Carl Fosberg of Point Pleasant, David Martin of Ventnor, Richard Sooy of Pleasantville, and John Zuback of Morgan. In the past few years, successful planked hulls have been used as molds for, or models for, fiberglass hulls.

The present speed skiff is 16 feet long with a 6-foot beam. Even though capable of high speeds, it is still usable and safe for limited offshore fishing. When throttled back from planing speed, it settles in as a safe displacement hull. In this unusual boat you can race at more than 60 M.P.H. one day and go fishing for blues or stripers the next.

Seaman introduced an outboard version of the speed skiff very early. These are 15 feet long and 6 feet wide. The sides are generally lower, unchanged from the early models. A Seaman innovation is a well for the motor, just forward of the transom, an important safety feature in a sea, and making a long shaft motor unnecessary. The outboard models were able to make speeds of 35 M.P.H. with the outboards available in 1940. With modern large outboards, speeds of 50 are possible. Seaman built about 100 of these skiffs up to 1956, when he reached the age of seventy-two.

The inboard speed skiff continues in active use, now in molded fiberglass, although a few planked hulls are still in use. A few examples of the outboard type are in use, and are highly prized by their owners. The latter deserve fabrication in fiberglass, as sporty able outboards, with local character and proud traditions.

SOURCES

Publications

Game Fish of the Pacific, Southern California and Mexico. George C. Thomas, Jr., and George C. Thomas III. Philadelphia, 1930.
American Big Game Fishing. New York, 1935.

Anecdotal Material

Daniel Ardolino, West Long Branch
Joseph E. Banfield, Ocean Township
George A. Frick, Neptune
Harold Kofoed, Keyport
John Luhrs, Red Bank
Capt. John Kocsik, Spring Lake Heights
Capt. George Mayer, Palm Beach, Fla.
Katherine R. Mayer, Palm Beach, Fla.
Harold A. Seaman, Port-au-Peck
Harry Van Sant, Atlantic City

An early Sea Bright skiff cruiser, 24 by 8 feet, built by Seaman for Jacob F. Oberle about 1915. *Courtesy of Harold A. Seaman.*

The *Dollie R.,* a 26-foot sea skiff cruiser built by Banfield, 1917–1918, powered by a 20-H.P., 4-cylinder Kermath engine. *Courtesy of Joseph A. Banfield.*

Here comes one of the "Sea Birds"

HENSLER-KOFOED COMPANY, INC.

SPECIFICATIONS

L. O. A: 19' 9"
BEAM: 6' 8"
DRAFT: 1' 8"
STEM: Sided   2"
BOTTOM: 1¼" white cedar, slip-tongued in seams, rabbitted to receive garboard.
TRANSOM: 1" mahogany over oak frames.
PLANKING: ¾" white cedar, lapstrake.
FRAMES: ⅞" x 1½" one piece steam-bent oak, spaced 6" centers.
FASTENINGS: Copper rivets, brass screws and bolts.
DECKS: Laminated fir covered with No. 10 canvas.
COVERING BOARD: Mahogany.
WINDSHIELD: Mahogany.
RAILS: Mahogany.
SISTER KEELSONS: 1¾" x 4" x 14', spaced to form engine bed.
FLOORS: White pine.
ENGINE COVER: Redwood.
BULKHEADS: Redwood.
STEERING GEAR: All brass, oversize rack steerer, rod connected.
RUDDER: Cast bronze, spade type.
SHAFT LOG: Cast bronze, self aligning.
PROPELLER SHAFT: 1" Tobin bronze.
PROPELLER: 3 blade Federal-Mogul.
STRUT: Bronze.
GAS TANK: 20 gallon capacity.
PAINT: Windshield, rails, covering board and transom varnished.
    Deck - Tan.
    Topsides - White.
    Bottom - Red anti-fouling copper.
    Interior - Light green.
    Floors - Dark green.
EQUIPMENT: Deck fittings all brass or bronze, one 8" cleat and two skene chocks forward; two 6" cleats mounted aft on each side; one combination bowlight and one pole type stern light, one 5 lb. navy type anchor, 80' x ½" anchor rope, two 20' dock lines, one automatic bilge bailer, one bilge pump, two life preservers, whistle, instrument panel including tachometer, oil and amper gauges, ignition and light switches, hand crank and sump pump.
PRICES: Complete, F. O. B., Keyport, New Jersey

	WINDSHIELD	WINDSHIELD & CANOPY
4-45 Gray	$1200.00	$1285.00
6-90 "	1350.00	1435.00
6-125 "	1500.00	1585.00

TOILET: $60.00 extra, including curtain.

Prices and specifications subject to change without notice.

HENSLER-KOFOED COMPANY, INC.

DESCRIPTION

There is a big flock of "Sea Birds" afloat, gratifying every sense of pleasure and contentment on the water.

After more than a quarter of a century of experience in building high grade sea skiffs, both large and small, the "Sea Bird" size and design was finally decided upon as filling a demand for a hull that is light, serviceable, economical and capable under any operating conditions.

While the equipment and power may be varied to suit an owner, the "one design" permits of duplication in pattern and perfection in detail that offers a buyer the greatest saving in cost that is consistent with our reputation for high grade work.

These boats make admirable tenders for large yachts because they are light, handy, strong and seaworthy.

Hensler-Kofoed Company, Inc.
156 Front Street
Keyport, New Jersey

SAFETY

- The "Sea Birds" Are Sea Skiffs -

The "Sea Birds" are light and bouyant and they plane over the seas instead of diving into them. Real sea ability is the factor of safety in the design.

Easy control at all speeds is assured by the light draft forward, which prevents "digging in" and "sheering about" and the spade rudder has bronze rack control with protection to the shaft, propeller and rudder provided by a full length keel.

COMFORT - STRENGTH

- The Sturdiest, Most Capable -

The "raised deck" type of design together with the generous beam, gives unusual width and freeboard for shelter, roominess and comfort when the going is rough.

An element of great strength lies in the construction of frame and planking which are all in one length without splices.

The planks are fitted, side lapped and copper riveted so that there need be no caulking and the sister keelsons run full length without splices to form the backbone and engine bed.

DEPENDABILITY

- And Reliable Sea Boats Known.

The "Sea Birds" come completely equipped, no extras to buy.

The "Sea Birds" are powered by Gray Marine Motors, Phantom Series. 45 H. P. - 125 H. P.

The speed is up to 38 M. P. H. selective.

The heavier the power the higher they "plane" up out of the water and lighten resistance.

"Sea Birds" are in regular service with the N. J. State Fish and Game Commission, an exacting service the year around on river, bay and off-shore.

[2 sides] Hensler Kofoed Sea Bird catalog, 1938. *Courtesy of Harold Kofoed.*

26 Foot Raised Deck Sea Skiff

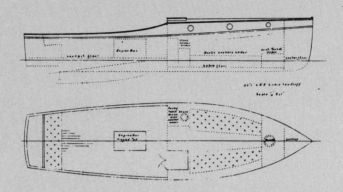

SPECIFICATIONS

L. O. A.: 26 feet.

BEAM: 6′ 8″.

BOTTOM: 2″ Spruce (Sliptongued in seams).

PLANKING: ⅝″ Select White Cedar (Lap-strake).

FRAMES: ¾″ x 1¼″ Oak (spaced 6″ centers).

FASTENINGS: Copper Rivets and Brass Screws.

FLOORS: ¾″ White Cedar T. & G. Painted.

BULKHEADS: Including berths and bulkheads in galley paneled and painted.

CABIN SIDES: White Cedar, 3 brass port lights with screens on each side.

DECKS: ⅜″ Laminated Fir covered with canvas and painted.

EQUIPMENT: 1 Sands Winner Toilet, 1 1-burner stove, 1 Ropeless Steerer (Brass), 1 Bronze Rudder, 1 Cleat, and 2 chocks forward, 1 Cleat and 2 chocks aft, 1 combination electric side light, 1 Electric Stern Light, 1 30-lb. Anchor (folding), 50′ of ½″ Anchor rope, 6 life preservers, fog horn and bell. 1 Dome Light in Cabin.

PAINT: 3 Coats (color optional).

PRICES

Price of Hull without Engine $..................................

PRICE COMPLETE WITH

		Speed	
Model F4	40–60 H.P. Scripps Marine Engine	17 M.P.H.	$..........................
Model F6	100 H.P. Scripps Marine Engine	22 M.P.H.	$..........................
Model G6	150 H.P. Scripps Marine Engine	28 M.P.H.	$..........................

Prices on other engines furnished upon application

Pages from Keyport Boat Works catalog, 1924. Note the relative speed and horsepower of the two models. *Courtesy of Harold Kofoed.*

36 Foot Trunk Cabin Sea Skiff

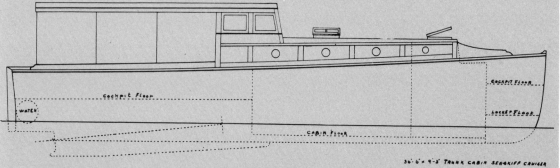

36'-6" x 9'-3" TRUNK CABIN SEA-SKIFF CRUISER

SPECIFICATIONS

L. O. A.: 36' 0".

BEAM: 9' 3".

HEADROOM IN CABIN AND AFT COCKPIT: 6' 2".

BOTTOM: 2" Spruce (Sliptongued in Seams).

SHAFT LOG: 4" Oak.

TRANSOM: 1" Mahogany.

SKAG: 4" Yellow Pine or Oak.

FRAMES: ⅞" x 1¾" Oak (spaced 6" centers).

PLANKING: ¾" White Cedar.

FASTENINGS: Copper Rivets and Brass Screws and Bolts.

CABIN: Trunk Cabin; Sides Mahogany, Deck, 1" T. & G. White Pine covered with canvas and painted, 4 brass Port lights with screens, 1 Skylight Mahogany frame, 1 hinged Hatch in Deck leading to forward cockpit.

CABIN EQUIPMENT: 1 Sands Winner Toilet, 1 Wash Basin, 1 Medicine Locker, 2 Stationary Berths with Lockers under, 2 Pullman Berths, 1 Dresser, 1 Clothes Locker, 1 Ice Box, 2 Pantry Lockers, 1 Galley Sink, 1 2-Burner Presto Lite Stove, Pullman cushions 3" Kapock covered with Khaki, Stationary Berths 5" Kapock covered with Khaki.

LIGHTS: 2 Electric Dome Lights in Cabin, 1 Electric Bulkhead fixture in Toilet, Electric Sailing Lights in Mahogany Light Boxes.

TRIM IN CABIN: Mahogany.

WINDSHIELD: Mahogany, Plate Glass Windows.

CANOPY TOP: Continuing from deck of Windshield, Decked with Laminated Fir and covered with Canvas, painted.

SEATS: 1 Seat in Aft Cockpit, 1 in Forward Cockpit, each with 3" Kapock Cushions. .

COVERING BOARD: ¾" T. & G. White Cedar (canvas covered).

FLOORING: 1" T. & G. Cedar covered with Linoleum.

PAINT: Inside and Outside 3 coats. Colors optional. All Mahogany stained and varnished 3 coats.

RUDDER: Brass and Kainer. Erico ropeless Steerer, Hyde Propeller, Bronze shaft and Stuffing box.

TANKS: 100-Gallon capacity Gasoline Tank. 50-Gallon Water Tank.

MOTOR INSTALLATION: All necessary fittings to make a first-class installation, such as copper exhaust line, Brass water connections, etc.

PRICES

Price of Hull Complete without Engine $..............................

PRICE COMPLETE WITH
Speed

100 H.P. "E" Scripps Marine Engine 15 M.P.H. $.............................

150 H.P. G6 Scripps Marine Engine 20 M.P.H. $.............................

Prices of other engines upon application.

A Kofoed Sea Bird under way. *Courtesy of Harold Kofoed.*

A Kofoed sea skiff cruiser. *Courtesy of Harold Kofoed.*

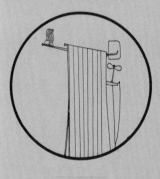

The New
KING "22" SPORT FISHERMAN

AFTER nearly 20 years of custom designing and building of practically every size and type of sea skiff, demand from seasoned boat owners for a small inexpensive craft, which will really perform in choppy seas and foul weather, has prompted us to bring this little ship to its present high standard of perfection.

Having originated this fast modern type of boat, and being the largest builders devoted exclusively to Sea Skiffs, we believe the new King "22" Sport Fisherman will be a "revelation" both in speed and extreme sea worthiness.

The uses to which a boat of this type can be put are many and varied. Having a turn of speed in excess of the average runabout, it is perfect for idling away a hot sultry afternoon; or with the shallow draft of the average outboard, to explore those out of the way places, far from dust and sign posts. With a sea-worthiness found in no other craft, it is ideal for off-shore fishing, or running the roughest inlets. As a racing yacht-tender for late fall duck hunting and many other purposes, this little craft has already proven its merit.

PATENT SPECIFICATIONS

KING PATENTS NO. 1,352,753
Pat. Sept. 14 1920.

A skiff having a hull with a keel terminating short of the stern and having the bilge forward of amidships bulging outwardly and outwardly and downwardly flattening toward the stern until it forms a transversely concave and rearwardly and downwardly inclined part where it overhangs the end of the keel.

These curvatures and the amount of curvature can be increased or diminished according to circumstances, but with a boat built in this way the very slight, much greater than with the ordinary skiff without the undue settling at the stern, and the form of the hull that permits this does not at all affect the sea worthiness of the boat.

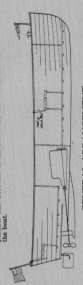

GENERAL ARRANGEMENT

Spacious forward deck allowing ample storage space underneath, with access from forward cockpit through large hinged hatch with lock and key provided. Large forward cockpit with seating arrangement as shown on plans or with option of seats extending along both sides. Water-proof engine hatch amidships with hinged mahogany top, giving easy access to motor. Spacious rear cockpit semi-self bailing with comfortable seat across stern. Steering is by means of bronze tiller at forward end of engine housing where all motor controls are brought for easy one-man operation. A comfortable upholstered seat with folding back rest is provided for driver.

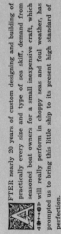

DETAILED SPECIFICATIONS

Length overall 22 feet.

Beam 6'-4"

Freeboard forward 3'-2"

Freeboard aft 2'-8"

Draft 20 inches.

Bottom—White spruce double planked 2 inches thick.

Planking—White boat cedar or mahogany 5/8".

Frames—White oak, one piece, steam bent, 7/8" x 1 1/2". Spacing between frames 7 1/2"

Stem—One piece straight grained white oak, 2 1/4" x 4".

Stern—Clear mahogany, 1 1/8" re-inforced with white oak across bottom and along sides.

Shoe—White oak 3 1/2" x 5" x 7 1/2 feet long, extending below propellor.

PRICE

Powered with 75 H. P. Chrysler Crown Marine Motor, Speed 30 M. P. H. _____ $1485. F. O. B. Factory.

TWO KING 28 FOOT SPEED SEA SKIFFS UNDERWAY.

DURING the past eighteen years that we have been custom builders of boats we have designed and constructed practically every size and type of sea skiff. Through this experience we have found that certain sizes and designs have proven to be more popular than others. Therefore it is only natural that in deciding to adopt our work to stock designs we should choose the models we have found to be the most popular.

The most popular of all these is our "28" Sportsman. This is a standard raised deck cruiser with protecting windshield amidships and large rear open co-kpit.

This model is arranged with forward toilet compartment separated from main cabin with partition and door, and with large sliding hatch overhead. Main cabin is fitted with two large upholstered berths with storage space under. Floors are covered with cork linoleum and cabin is lighted with two electric dome lights overhead.

Galley is separated from main cabin with half high partitions and is fully equipped with large capacity ice box, galley sink and pump, large storage locker and two burner stove and with dish rack built in overhead. Interior of cabin is trimmed with mahogany.

Windshield is of mahogany and glass, and extends back over motor, giving complete protection to driving compartment. Forward sashes are of heavy glass and open outward on quadrants. Motor is housed under removable water tight compartment with flat mahogany top which serves as seat or chart holder. After end of engine box is slatted to allow bilge ventilation. All controls are brought forward to steering position and are housed in mahogany control box. Large open after cockpit with floor covering exhaust pipe, steering gear, etc., and with large upholstered seat across stern.

The installation of motor is performed with best available materials such as copper exhaust, brass water pipe, copper gasoline tanks, all brass and bronze rudder and all necessary equipment to complete the job.

Three coats of yacht white are applied to outside of hull with anti-fouling green copper below water line. Inside of cabin is in flat white and rear cockpit in light grey. All mahogany such as cabin sides, windshield and trim inside and out is left bright and finished with best grade spar varnish.

We have exercised unusual care in the construction of the hulls for our sportsman models incorporating many features that we have found from experience to make a dry seaworthy boat. A slight V or flare in the bow at the water line curls down the water instead of allowing it to roll up the sides and be blown over the water instead of one length and are shiplapped and riveted before being set up, making it impossible for them to dry open and leak, instead of the usual method of joining the bottom plank with a slip tongue which often splits, making it necessary to caulk or swell before launching. All butts below water line are scarfed and riveted through and through, instead of the usual square cut.

The transom is re-inforced with oak along each side and across bottom and the bottom itself is double planked above propeller and rudder. All planking is of the best grade mahogany. Frames are of one piece steam bent white oak. The stern log, dead wood, stem, and all other re-inforcing are also of white oak. Copper rivets over copper burrs and heavy brass screws are used for fastening in planking, and heavy brass bolts are used through bed frames, stern log, etc., no iron being used anywhere in hull to cause rust and leakage.

SPECIFICATIONS OF SPORTSMAN 28'

Beam	8' 6"
Draught	24"
Freeboard for'd	5' 2"
Freeboard aft	3' 1"
Bottom spruce	2" x 28"
Frames white oak	7/8 x 1¾"
Spaced center to center	9"
Planking mahogany	¾"
Transom mahogany	1¼"
Stern log, dead wood shoe etc., white oak	4"
Propellor shaft everdur.	1⅛"
Stern bearing	Heavy bronze
Stuffing box	Inside-bronze
Steering gear	Worm gear ropeless
Gasoline tanks copper	70 gal.
Ice box capacity	75 lbs.
Water capacity	25 gal.
Sleeping accommodations (option)	2 or 4

EQUIPMENT

Life preservers	1
Anchor	1
Anchor line	1
Fire extinguisher	1
Fog Horn	1
Fog bell	1
Porcelain toilet	1
Enameled galley sink	1
Running lights (electric)	4
Two burner alcohol stove	1
Name & license	yes
Pilot Rules	yes

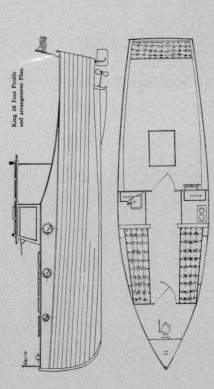

King 28 Foot Profile
and arrangement Plan.

King Boat Works catalog.

The boat that popularized the Sea Bright skiff beyond home waters, the Banfield of about 1928. *Courtesy of Joseph A. Banfield.*

A 32-foot sea skiff cruiser built by Pierre Proal at Red Bank about 1929. It was powered by a single 200-H.P. Hall-Scott engine. *Courtesy of George A. Frick.*

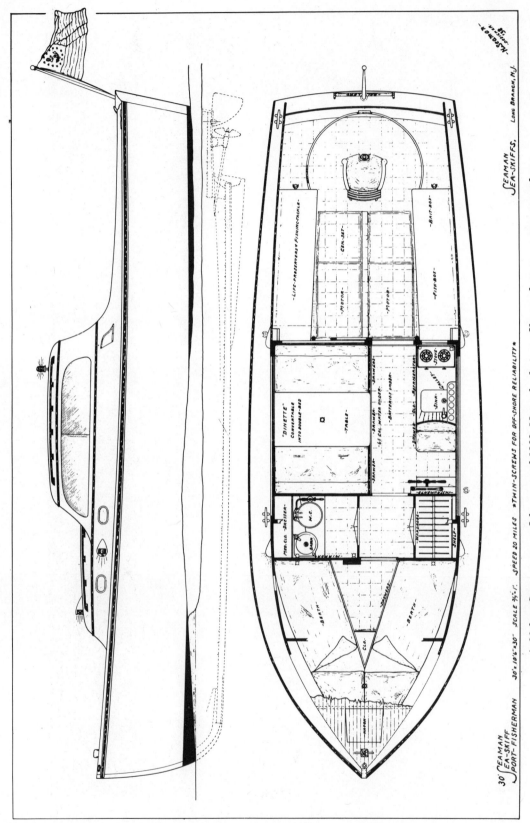

A 30-foot Seaman sport fisherman of 1938. Note the low profile, modern appearance, and excellent interior arrangement. A box or rolled garboard design was still used. *Courtesy of Harold A. Seaman.*

A 31-foot Ulrichsen trunk cabin cruiser, typical of the modern skiff. *Courtesy of John Luhrs.*

The *P.J.*, first of the speed skiffs built by Seaman in 1922, attained a speed of 21 M.P.H. with 20 H.P. *Courtesy of Harold A. Seaman.*

The last skiff built by Seaman, a 16-foot outboard speed skiff. *Courtesy of Harold A. Seaman.*

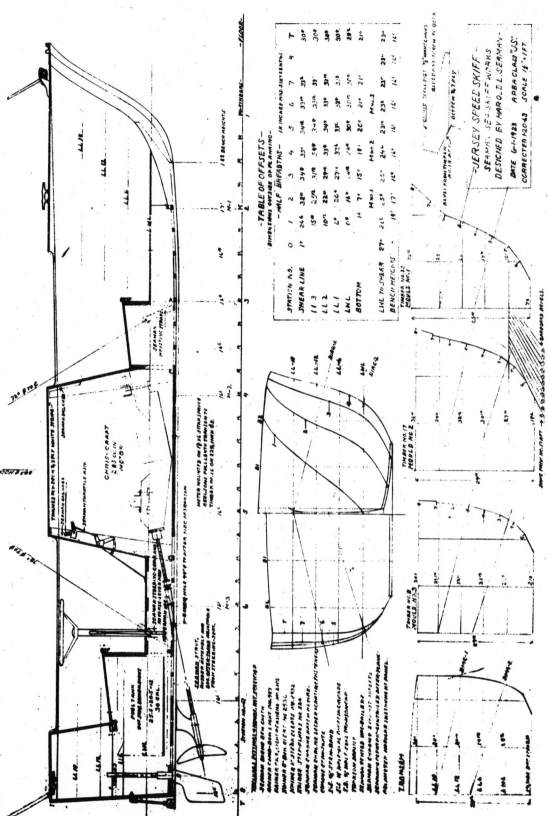

Lines of Seaman's Jersey Speed Skiff. *Courtesy of Harold A. Seaman.*

8

The Sea Skiff Builders

The study of the builders has been largely confined to those men constructing beach skiffs, surf boats, pound boats, and other variants of the basic Sea Bright skiff design. There were other contemporary builders of sloops, schooners, yachts, and steam vessels, who have been omitted. A number of the skiff builders constructed other types as well, particularly in the later years.

Information on the life and work of most builders is extremely sparse. The census records of 1850, 1860 and 1870 are often of value, particularly if the builder is cited in Schedule 5 as a manufacturer. Commercial and local business directories may indicate the type of vessel and location of the boat yard. However, omission may mean nothing except failure of the individual to subscribe, or the salesman to call. A great deal of the data is anecdotal, an acceptable term for hearsay history. Very few builders left plans, account books, correspondence or firmly identified models. Many of the models have found their place as ornaments, their history being completely lacking or occasionally the product of romantic fancy.

Early city and township records, local tax rolls, and surveys have been largely unproductive. Some county atlases and town maps have been very helpful in showing locations of yards.

The anecdotal data have been obtained from principals, former employers, former employees, associates, friends, enemies, and competitors. There is substantial agreement from the many informants but dates may be somewhat variable. The amount of data reflects the impression made by the builder on his peers rather than his technical contribution. An occasional builder of supreme ability may be remembered by little more than name and location whereas a colorful near incompetent may be known and remembered by many, thirty years after his demise. A few builders' works and accomplishments have been preserved when succeeded in the same location by a former employee or sons. In these rare cases, data may be more easily secured and analyzed.

Designs were characteristic of the times, and highly individual from builder to builder. It was formerly possible to recognize the work of each local builder who usually had too much pride to borrow obvious features from a competitor. He was likely to adapt good construction features or the use of new materials, but these had to represent real progress, not an alteration in appearance for the sake of novelty or eye appeal.

Over a period of years a builder would evolve a set of lines to fit the needs of a particular service, or a group of commercial users. He might favor a straight stem, little flare forward, a straight sheer, wide transom, flat bottom, and transom without tumble home. These produced a relatively fast, flat-riding, but somewhat wild skiff. Another favored a more buoyant bow with marked flare, greater sheer, a rounded bottom, producing a slower but more sea-kindly boat. The customer made a choice depending upon his needs for speed, seaworthiness needed in negotiating a particular inlet, and in relation to his estimate of his own seamanship. Fishermen had a great capacity for practical judgments, sometimes not shared by the yachtsman.

Most builders made half models and a few made plans as well. The builders who worked from plans usually made a trial half model to check the smoothness of contours before construction.

The builders' names have been listed in alphabetical order. The data are so scant that in some cases only name, location and the time in which he worked or flourished, is known. In one case, the first name is not definitely known.

Carl Adams, Smithville. From about 1900 to the present. Built a great variety of boat types from gunning skiffs and commercial fishermen to sea skiffs of varying pattern.

James Adams, Morgan. Employed by the Keyport Marine Railway. Banfield and Humphries yards. Established a boat shop on the north shore of Morgan Creek about 1932 where skiffs were built until 1940.

Nils Anderson, Keyport. Formerly employed by the Kofoed yard. Constructed skiffs at several locations to 1950.

Joseph E. Banfield, Leonardo, Atlantic Highlands. Started a boat shop in Leonardo in 1914, moving to Atlantic Highlands in a few years. His boats were immediately successful because of advanced design and efficient methods. During the war he built a number of skiffs as dispatch boats, for government use. In the postwar years, standard 32- and 38-foot skiffs were built on an assembly line, from precut pieces. Many skilled local builders were employed, at wages higher than they could make if self-employed. A total of 5,000 skiffs were built and the number of employees was 120 during the peak. The firm went into receivership in 1930 and the plant burned in 1938. Banfield was largely responsible for the increased popularity of the sea skiff in distant areas.

Abraham Bartholomew, Sea Bright. Beach skiffs prior to World War I. Later employed by Banfield.

David Beaton, West Mantoloking. Emigrated from Scotland, and employed by Hubert Johnson of Bay Head. Established his own yard in 1925. Constructed skiffs up to 1938. Construction of small sailing craft thereafter.

Jack Benson, Beach Haven. Constructed utility skiffs and pound boats from 1920 to 1940.

Sigurd Benson was employed as a foreman at the Hankins boat works in Lavalette. He later built skiffs and pound boats at Manasquan, Osbornville, and other locations from 1920 to 1935.

Walter J. Bennett, Neptune. Previously employed as a foreman by Banfield and others. Built skiffs from 1920 to 1932.

Paul Berthelime, Keyport. Sports skiffs 1945 to 1950.

Neill Campbell was born near Shark River in 1865. He was apprenticed to a boat builder on the Shrewsbury River, returning to Belmar to set up a boat shop about 1900. He constructed beach skiffs, rowboats, sneak boxes, gunning skiffs, sloops, and commercial fishing boats. In addition, he operated a boat livery, and at one time, a restaurant called the Hong Kong Inn. A son, Robert J., was born in 1891 and was active in the business, succeeding Neill who died in 1945. He was in turn succeeded by his sons Donald M. and Robert D. about 1937, although he lived until 1957. The two sons have continued the business to the present, although construction of boats was discontinued about 1962. Luckily, a large number of half models have been preserved, and are easily identifiable. A number were never built, representing only the builders' thoughts in solid form. Photographs of Sea Bright skiff hulls were included in the chapter on other fishing types, to illustrate a half century of development. There are a number of file-bottom or deadrise half models. A typical, and commonly used, model is for a boat 18 by 5½ feet. These were rigged as sloops or cats and were popular as party or charter boats. There is a larger similar model for a hull 24 by 7½ feet. Another half model has an identical profile and dimensions, but has a round bilge instead of the less expensive chine design. There are several other models for boats 15½ by 6 feet, in both round bilge and chine design which represent an attempt to establish a local class of small sailboats. Examples of these were in use to the late 1930's. The lines of some of these are reminiscent of some small planing sailboats. Campbell built numbers of sneak-box pattern, and other, gunning skiffs. The boxes were 12 by 4 feet and a stock of one or two was always on hand for sale. Some other models were the work of Robert J., a work bateau, a V-bottom runabout, several rowing bateaus for the boat livery, a step sea skiff, and commercial fishermen.

The Campbell boat shop consisted of a central assembly area surrounded by a circular saw, band saw and planer. A steam box was connected to a boiler and was used to make the white oak frames, and occasionally cedar or mahogany planking, flexible. A long bench was provided for shaping and assembly of smaller sections. Forms and patterns were stored on the floor or in the loft. One area of the floor was painted white for use in lofting. All facilities for construction of a boat to 40 feet were provided in one building, dependent upon the skills of the experienced builder.

Lars Christianson, Keyport area before 1916.

Robert A. Clark, Point Pleasant, flourished about 1870.

Joseph V. Clayton, Union Beach and Keansburg, from 1924 to present. Small fishing skiffs.

Charles Cliamont, Lawrence Harbor. Built fishing skiffs and other types. He originated his own type of box garboard. Flourished 1919 to 1943.

William Clock, Port Monmouth, flourished about 1870.

William Delaney, Keyport, sports fishing skiffs, in recent years.

Edwin Dennis, Long Branch. Born in 1813 and flourished before and during the Civil War.

William A. Douglass, Riceville, now Navesink village. Flourished about 1870.

Robert Emery, Long Branch. Flourished about 1880.

Carl Forsberg, Point Pleasant. Formerly employed by Hubert Johnson. Sea skiffs, including speed skiffs from 1946.

A. Hanaway, Manasquan. Flourished about 1870.

Charles Hankins, Lavalette. Formerly employed by Huff in Long Branch. Established his own business about 1906. Built surf boats, beach skiffs and pound boats. Was succeeded by his son. The firm continues to build beach skiffs which are used for patrolling swimming beaches. They also build excellent box garboard skiffs from 22 to 32 feet in length.

Jacob Herbert, Manasquan. Built surf boats for the Life Saving Service as well as beach skiffs. He was born in 1832 and flourished about 1870.

John H. Hendrickson, Long Branch. Built small skiffs and intermittently was employed by Seaman. Flourished from 1900 to about 1923.

Howard Hoffman, Belmar. Began building pound boats about 1902. Continued in business to 1928 when succeeded by his son Harold L., who moved to Brielle. Harold continued to build skiffs until 1940.

Charles P. Huff was born in England in 1821. He was employed in the Williamsburg yard of William Webb before coming to Long Branch about 1869. Sons, Charles H. and George W., were born in 1856 and 1859. They worked with their father, taking over the shop on his death in 1907. They continued in active business to 1922. Their production was confined to beach skiffs, small pound boats, and an occasional surf boat. The Huffs had a reputation for integrity and care, their boats having a life of five or ten years longer than many of their competitors. Their skiffs had a comparatively wider bottom plank than those of other builders. The Huffs customarily did not employ power tools, to avoid scorching. At least one seventy-year-old Huff skiff is still in existence.

E. Fell Jardine, Atlantic City. Built a number of skiffs of the Sea Bright pattern following World War I. Several were for the Coast Guard.

Hubert Johnson, Bay Head. Son of Morton Johnson. Had an early interest in gasoline engines which led him to establish his own yard about 1915. He produced a line of fast sports fishing skiffs of superior design and finish from about 1930. He died in 1949 but the yard continues to the present.

Morton Johnson, Bay Head. Was employed by his father William, a boat builder, before establishing a shop about 1880. He built beach skiffs and pound boats but his principal work was in small sailboats, power boats and fine yachts. He died in 1933 but the yard continues to the present.

The Johnson brothers, Zack and Abraham, established a yard in Bay Head about 1924. They produced many fine sports-fishing skiffs. A successor continues the yard.

Abram Joralemon was a Jersey City boat builder who came to Monmouth Beach about 1885. He established a shop next to the ice houses of the Galilee fishermen. He built beach skiffs and pound boats as well as sailboats and fine yachts. His son Willard H. was born in Jersey City in 1885, and continued the business until his death in 1950. He was followed by his son Harold C. In the late 1940's, small sports-fishing skiffs were built. The business was taken over by Andrew Ulrichsen about 1950.

Stewart B. King, formerly a fisherman, started building skiffs at Highlands about 1903 during the winter off season. With the advent of power, his boats proved fast and were used by local lobstermen. A patent was issued to him in 1920, as noted in the chapter on other fishing types. He was succeeded by his sons George G. and Lester L., and finally grandsons Stewart and Phillip who have continued the business.

Holger Kofoed, Keyport. Kofoed had been trained as a naval architect in Denmark. About 1910 he established a boat shop in Sea Bright, where beach skiffs and pound boats were built. In 1918 he moved to a new and larger yard on the creek in Keyport. Here he produced commercial skiffs, cruisers, rum runners and Sea Birds. Gilbert Hensler of Newark had a financial interest from 1928 to 1934. The yard continued to the end of World War II.

Jesse Laber, Long Branch. Flourished about 1870.

H. C. Lane, Long Branch. Flourished about 1870.

Henry Luhrs, Morgan. Formerly worked with Cliamont and Kofoed, who encouraged Luhrs. Established his own yard at Morgan about 1931. In 1940 he pioneered a 21-foot sport skiff, a development of the Sea Bird type, which was an immediate success. He now produces a large number of medium-size sports skiffs.

Harry Maddox was employed in lobstering and as captain of a party boat during the summer, and as a skiff builder during the off season. He constructed excellent skiffs up to 28 feet in his shop at 1031 Monroe Ave. in Asbury Park from 1905 to 1939. His production was one to four boats yearly.

John Mahr, Long Branch. Built pound boats and beach skiffs prior to 1916. He was later employed as a foreman by Seaman.

William Morris, Long Branch. Flourished before the Civil War.

John Mount and Charles Williams, Long Branch. Started on Troutman's Creek near Atlantic Avenue before 1905. They built commercial skiffs, yachts, and sailboats, at various locations to World War II.

Ralph Mulford, Rumson. Formerly an automobile racer, built small power skiffs resembling the Seaman speed skiff in the old Nelson and Benson shop from 1930. During World War II he was superintendent of the Elco motor torpedo boat plant at Bayonne.

Andrew Nelson and Nils Benson, Rumson Point. Built beach skiffs and commercial fishing boats from 1900 to 1925. They also built bateaus and garveys for shad fishermen.

Lawrence B. Newman started a boat shop on River Road in Pleasure Bay before 1873. He constructed pound boats on a standard model which was not modified during his entire life. A sketch of the sections of a Seaman pound boat in comparison with a Newman boat are shown in the section on pound boats. He produced a sufficient

number so that one or two boats were always on hand for sale, an unusual business departure during those years, and one that rewarded
the builder. Newman also built surf boats for the Life Saving Service
and may have had a shop in Manasquan at one time. He continued in
business to World War I.

Olav Olsen, Keyport. Formerly employed by Kofoed. Started his
own shop about 1947. Produces pleasure and commercial skiffs from
22 to 30 feet.

S. Bartley Pearce, Brielle. Was the son of Shem B., a Civil War
veteran born about 1835, and a builder of local schooners, beach skiffs,
and sloops. S. Bartley was born about 1860, and started his own yard
about 1883. His designs were conceived in the wood, as half models.
Fortunately, some of these are preserved by his family, including one
of a Manasquan River schooner, probably from his father. S. Bartley
built surf boats and pound boats, as well as sloops, sneakboxes, and
small sailboats. A group of the latter were sailed by the Manasquan
River Yacht Club before 1910. Pearce was also a pioneer motor boat
racer, representing the U.S. in early Harmsworth races. He was recognized for his ingenuity, excellent design, and ability to conceive, design, build and handle anything from a small sailboat, racing boat, to
a large yacht. He retired about 1928 but continued to build small
rowing bateaus as a hobby until his death in 1933.

Hans Petersen, Keyport. Formerly employed by Kofoed, he established his own shop in 1934. He has been succeeded by his sons Eric
and Ian. They produce up to ten or twelve high-grade commercial and
pleasure skiffs annually.

Pierre Proal, Red Bank. Was the proprietor of the Red Bank
Yacht Works between the two world wars. He produced a variety of
skiffs including rum runners, yachts to 45 feet, and commercial boats.

William Ryan, Neptune. Sports skiffs, 1945 to 1955.

South Jersey Shipbuilding Company, Atlantic City. Produced
skiffs of Sea Bright and South Jersey pattern, principally before World
War II.

Charles F. Strickland, Beach Haven. Has built pound boats and commercial skiffs of varying size to the present.

Isaac Seaman was a seasonal fisherman at Nauvoo, prior to the Civil War. He made his way by water from his home at Pamropo, the present Bayonne, each spring and returned in the fall. He constructed beach skiffs in the off season and was succeeded by his son Walter A. from 1859 to 1883, and by his grandson, William A., who was the proprietor of the boat yard from 1879 to 1929. He was in turn followed by Harold who has continued to build boats to the age of eighty-three, in 1965. Many of the innovations in design were made by the Seamans. The term sea skiff appears first in their advertisements in 1875, and Harold originated the Jersey speed skiff.

Howard Terry, West Keansburg. Built small commercial skiffs from about 1925 to 1950. His family had operated a shipyard in Keyport which produced large vessels and steamboats before 1860.

Andrew Ulrichsen was formerly employed by Kofoed. He established a boat shop in Keyport, then acquired the Joralemon shop in Monmouth Beach about 1950. He was associated with Wilson for a short time. The business was acquired by others before its removal to Marlboro in 1959.

Jacob Vaughn, Forked River. Produced surf boats for the Life Saving Service, beach skiffs, and sloops. Flourished after 1870.

Dorey Ware, Osbornville. Built pound boats and commercial skiffs from 1915 to 1940.

Harry Whitlock and Edward Waite, Neptune. Built pleasure and commercial skiffs 24 to 35 feet in length from 1923 to 1932.

George Williams, Leonardo. Commercial skiffs before 1945.

Hans W. Wulf, Red Bank. Small numbers of sports skiffs prior to 1940.

Harry L. Zobel established a boat yard at Sea Bright about 1925. Small and medium sized sports skiffs were built, reminiscent of the Sea Birds. The Zobels were good performers and were well built. The business was sold in 1932, and was moved to Red Bank following a fire in the mid 1950's.

John Zuback, Morgan. Had originally been employed by Cliamont. He established his own shop about 1947, producing high grade sports skiffs and fast speed skiffs.

Nearly a century and a half have passed since the birth of the Sea Bright skiff. At first glance, there is little similarity between it and present models. However, a stage by stage study demonstrates the orderly progression and development.

Construction and business practices have altered radically, more so than the boat itself. Formerly the customer selected the builder who best satisfied his requirements for skill, proximity, model, reputation, and price. A boat was then constructed to order, or was modified from a standard model to meet needs.

Today, the mass production methods of the automobile industry produce excellent boats, usually built at distant points, widely advertised and merchandised, and sold locally by retail dealers who are adept in terms of trade-in sales and bank financing.

The success of mass production depends upon reducing a complicated structure into its relatively simple elements, each of which can be performed adequately by a properly trained and supervised but unskilled worker. The use of fiberglass and plastics requires technical knowledge in new fields and large capital. The ultimate product is often excellent but is occasionally the host of a series of minor omissions, defects, and oversights in supervision.

The few surviving individual boat builders will continue to flourish as long as there are equally individualistic and demanding boatmen.

S. Bartley Pearce boat shop at Brielle about 1905. Note the "deadrise" sloop at the dock and the pound boat at far right. *Courtesy of Mrs. H. H. Kroh.*

A sloop, similar to half model shown on the following page, under construction in the Pierce boat shop, about 1905. *Courtesy of Mrs. H. H. Kroh.*

S. Bartley Pearce "thinking in the wood," about 1920. Three or four models were often made and altered from a set of plans. The designer's fingers were more sensitive than the shape of the diagonals on the plan. *Courtesy of Mrs. H. H. Kroh.*

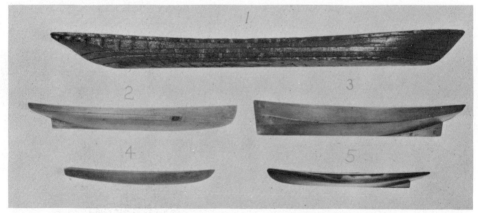

Pearce half models: 1. A shoal draft schooner of a type in general use in the shallow New Jersey inlets, probably by Shem B. Pearce about 1870. 2. Hull usually rigged as a sloop or catboat. The same model was later modified by hanging the rudder on the transom. (See photograph of hull under construction on the preceding page.) 3. Deadrise hull, formerly rigged as a sloop or catboat. It was later used for power boats. 4. Sneakbox. 5. Small sloop or catboat, similar to some built for members of the Manasquan Yacht Club. *Courtesy of Mrs. H. H. Kroh.*

Views of Seaman boat shop. *Courtesy of Harold A. Seaman.*

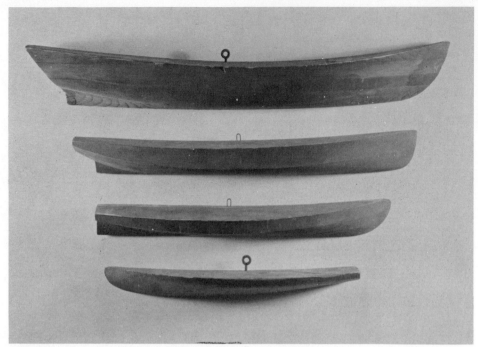

Campbell half models: From above, a 22-foot beach skiff, about 1905; an 18-foot deadrise sloop or catboat, 1905; a 15½-foot deadrise sloop or catboat, said to have been an early local "class," about 1900; a 13¼-foot sloop or catboat reminiscent of a sneakbox, about 1900.

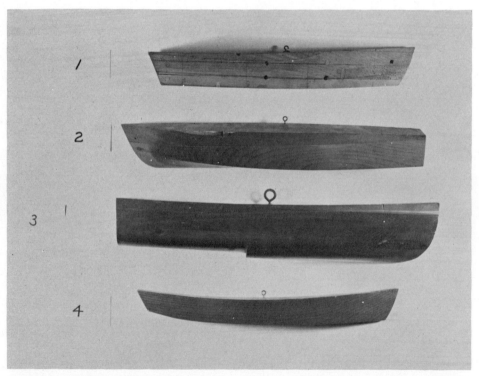

Later Campbell half models: 1. A 15½-foot work bateau, usually powered with a Model T Ford engine. 2. A 17-foot, 9-inch, vee-bottom runabout, built about 1930. 3. A 19-foot "step" sea skiff, a variation of a fast lobster boat. It was never built. 4. A 15½-foot rowing bateau of the type used in the boat livery from 1920 to 1940. They rowed very easily.

II The Barnegat Sneakbox and Other Shore Boats

1

The Barnegat Sneakbox and Nathaniel Bishop

The sneakbox is widely known, Nathaniel Bishop forgotten; yet an account of the boat is incomplete without one of the man who popularized it.

Nathaniel Holmes Bishop III, native of Medford, Massachusetts, voyager, pioneer canoeist, and New Jersey cranberry grower, made the boating and sporting world conscious of the merits of the unique craft.

In 1855, at the age of seventeen, he hiked across lower South America. The lively and intelligent account, *The Pampas and Andes: A Thousand Mile Walk Across South America,* was published in 1869. Bishop came to Ocean County, New Jersey, before 1864, establishing himself as a cranberry grower near Hanover. He had moved to Manahawkin, close to Barnegat Bay, by 1872. Here he became interested in the sport of canoeing, newly introduced into the United States from Great Britain. He ordered construction of a light, cedar-planked canoe by J. S. Lamson of Bordentown, N.J. The 18-foot, lap-strake hull, complete with oars, sail, mast and rudder, weighed 300 pounds. He named the canoe *Mayeta,* and started a voyage south from Quebec. The

Mayeta proved too heavy and was replaced by a 58-pound paper canoe constructed by Elisha Waters and Sons of Troy, N.Y. This was named *Maria Theresa* and carried Bishop to Florida in 1874–75 along the inland waterways of the Atlantic coast. The engaging account, *Voyage of the Paper Canoe,* was published in 1878.

Interest in canoes and proximity to Barnegat Bay brought the sneakbox to his attention. He became interested to the extent of owning and using five of them by 1875. He then commissioned the construction of the *Centennial Republic,* a twelve-foot sneakbox, by George Bogert of Manahawkin. It was used by Bishop in a voyage from Pittsburgh to Florida by way of the Ohio and Mississippi Rivers. On his return from this voyage the *Centennial Republic* was exhibited at the Centennial Exhibition in Philadelphia, and later at the Smithsonian Institution.

Bishop's trip produced his third book, *Four Months in a Sneak-Box,* published in 1879. The widely read and quoted book was responsible for the rapid spread of knowledge and interest in this new craft. It is important to us for its history of the development of the sneakbox.

The first step is attributed to Hazelton Seaman of West Creek, a boat builder and expert gunner, who had been born in New Jersey about 1807. He conceived and built a low, light, decked gunning skiff for his own use about 1836. He called this boat of unusual design a "devil's coffin." The local baymen were impressed with its air of stealth and concealment, calling it a "sneak-box" or "sneak boat." The model was soon borrowed and modified by others. Seaman's canvas spray screen on the forward deck was supported by an oaken hoop. This was improved in the second sneakbox, constructed a short time later by John Cranmer, Jr. The third was built with other modifications by Samuel Perrine, boat builder of the town of Barnegat. By 1875 the design had matured, attaining near perfection. J. Howard Perrine built at least forty different sizes and models of the sneakbox. He referred to the larger ones as "melonseeds."

Bishop, in his influential book, gives credit to Charles Hallock for publication of a description and drawings of the Sneakbox in *Forest and Stream* magazine of April 23, 1874. This appears to be in the form of a letter from Robert B. White dated April 3, 1874, at Shrewsbury. The diagram shows the center board trunk at the side of the cockpit, about ten inches off center, a common feature in later models.

A description of Bishop's boat is typical of contemporary craft. Length is 12 feet and beam 4 feet. The bottom is curved on nearly a smooth arc, as is the deck on a considerably larger radius. The bow is spoon-shaped and shallow. The transom is not raked, and is low and wide. The broad beam and shallow draft produce a stable hull which sails and rows well, traveling over and not through the water. There is no sheer and the high-cambered deck produces a profile with apparent reverse sheer. There is a central, rectangular cockpit with raised coaming and removable cover. The cockpit is protected by a triangular canvas apron on the foredeck, stretched upward on a 2-foot long stick. The shallow rudder is controlled by a yoke, or "cross tiller" and lines. The narrow 3-foot daggerboard passes through a narrow, midships well, forward of the cockpit. The rig is a low spritsail on a short, un-stayed mast. The local white cedar was used in construction. Straight-grained wood was used for planking and wood with curved grain was used for knees, frames, and carlins. Frames were $1\frac{1}{4}$ inches sawn, as were carlins. The bottom planking was $\frac{1}{2}$ inch in thickness and at least 6 inches in width. The deck planking was the same thickness, at least 7 inches in width, and was tongue and grooved. This added substantially to strength and rigidity. Both deck and bottom planking are but slightly tapered toward the ends. All planks are fastened aft to the transom and forward to a harpin, or horizontal member, at sheer level. The bottom is protected from wear by two narrow oak strips, or shoes. A completely finished and rigged sneakbox of first class construction cost from $65 to $75 and a poor one could be obtained for $25. Bishop's *Centennial Republic* cost $75 including oars, sail, spars, anchor, etc. The diagram from Bishop's Book gives an excellent and detailed rendering.

At this point we have an established and unique boat type, the further development of which will be followed in later chapters.

In the meantime, Nathaniel Bishop continued his marine interests, an interest in nature, and a sense of interest and responsibility in the welfare of his fellow townsmen.

He had moved to a house on Water Street in Toms River, on the wooded river bank. A neighbor, Mrs. Zulima Woodward, remembers him when she was a child. He was very quiet, well liked, slight, erect and had reddish hair and beard. He appeared taller because of his carriage. He was often at work on his boats and canoes and had two kayaks in the backyard. Reuben Corlies, Manahawkin boat builder, still recollects Bishop's interest in boats. He continued to write about canoes in *Forest and Stream* and later in *The American Canoeist,* corresponding with other interested people here and abroad. About 1878 he suggested a common organization be established of the numerous separate canoe clubs. He continued to promote union. An organization meeting was held on Lake George at Crosbyside Park in 1880 at which the American Canoe Association was formed. Bishop was the first secretary, filling the post to 1886 and compiling its early yearbook.

Bishop continued experimenting and combining the features of canoe and sneakbox into a hybrid which anticipated the features of the *Gloriana* of Nathaniel Herreshoff.

As noted before, Bishop had come to New Jersey before 1864, entering the field of cranberry culture which had been introduced from Cape Cod about 1855. By 1900, he had bought, sold, leased or rented sixty-one properties, including his home and a cemetery plot. In addition to his Toms River home, he owned property at Caldwell on Lake George, in Monrovia, California, and on Lake Worth in Florida. He was appreciative of the natural beauty of all these sites but considered Toms River second to none.

Bishop's last contribution and gesture came as a surprise to his fellow townsmen of Toms River. He died suddenly in 1902 while in Lake George and was buried in Riverside Cemetery in Toms River, beside his wife. The holographic will was characteristic of its author in detail and tone. After providing for his sister-in-law, the residua went to the Township of Dover for a public library. He indicated that the bequest was on behalf of himself and his wife, constituting the savings of a lifetime. The will provided for a fireproof building, selection of a rotating governing board of three men and two women, and it prohibited certain types of books. These were books of an immoral nature, disrespectful of women, of the marriage vows, of family rights and virtues, or tending to make divorce acceptable to the young. To the mothers of the township was assigned the duty of deciding what should be excluded, to protect purity and morality. In addition, the will bound the Township of Dover to perpetual care of the burial plot of Bishop and his wife.

Bishop selected his old friend Bernard Hainer, a Toms River pharmacist, and his wealthy brother Heber R. Bishop of New York as executors, the latter as financial advisor, the former to be paid for his services. The initial value of the fund was $12,913.18. This increased to $77,996.05 at the time of final accounting on November 22, 1935. The library, on Main Street in Toms River, was erected and finally dedicated on January 16, 1941.

The following is Bishop's description of his boat, quoted from *Four Months in a Sneak-box:*

To find such a boat—one that possessed many desirable points in a small hull—had been with me a study of years. I commenced to search for it in my boyhood—twenty-five years ago; and though I have carefully examined numerous small boats while travelling in seven foreign countries, and have studied the models of miniature craft in museums, and at exhibitions of marine architecture, I failed to discover the object of my desire, until, on the sea-shore of New Jersey, I saw for the first time what is known among gunners as the Barnegat sneak-box.

Having owned, and thoroughly tested in the waters of Barnegat and Little Egg Harbor bays, five of these boats, I became convinced that their claims for the good-will of the boating fraternity had not been over-estimated; so when I planned my second voyage from northern America to the Gulf of Mexico, and selected the great water-courses of the west and south (the Ohio and Mississippi rivers) as the route to be explored and studied, I chose the Barnegat sneak-box as the most comfortable model combined with other advantages for a voyager's use.

.   .   .   .

The peculiar advantages of the sneak-box were known to but few of the hunting and shooting fraternity, and, with the exception of an occasional visitor, were used only by the oystermen, fishermen, and wild-fowl shooters of Barnegat and Little Egg Harbor bays, until the New Jersey Southern Railroad and its connecting branches penetrated to the eastern shores of New Jersey, when educated amateur sportsmen from the cities quickly recognized in the little gunning-punt all they had long desired to combine in one small boat.

.   .   .   .

. . . The water-lines of the sneak-box are peculiar, and differ materially from those of row-boats, sailboats, and yachts. Having a spoon-shaped bottom and bow, the sneak-box moves rather over the water than through it, and this peculiarity, together with its broad beam, gives the boat such stiffness that two persons may stand upright in her while she is moving through the water, and troll their lines while fishing, or discharge their guns, without careening the boat; a valuable advantage not possessed by our best cruising canoes.

The boat sails well on the wind, though hard to pull against a strong head sea. A fin-shaped centre-board takes the place of a keel. It can be quickly removed from the trunk, or centre-board well, and stored under the deck. The flatness of her floor permits the sneak-box to run in very shallow water while being rowed or when sailing before the wind without the centre-board. Some of these boats, carrying a weight of three hundred pounds, will float in four to six inches of water.

SOURCES

Publications

Bishop, Nathaniel H. *The Pampas and Andes: A Thousand Mile Walk Across South America.* Boston, 1869.
———. *Voyage of the Paper Canoe.* Boston, 1878.
———. *Four Months in a Sneak-Box.* Boston, 1879.
Beers, Comstock and Kline. *A Topographic Map of Ocean County, 1872.*
U.S. Census Records of 1850.
Obituary, *New Jersey Courier,* July 10, 1902.

Unpublished Material

Last Will and Testament, Nathaniel H. Bishop. Hall of Records, Ocean County, New Jersey.
Index of Deeds. Hall of Records, Ocean County, New Jersey.
Historical Records, American Canoe Association.

Personal Reminiscences and Anecdotal Material

Mrs. Pauline S. Miller, title searcher and historian, Toms River
Mrs. Zulima Woodward, Toms River
Ronald M. Hoffman, Department of Physical Education, St. Lawrence University, Canton, N.Y.
Mrs. Elizabeth Morgan, Toms River
Reuben Corlies, Manahawkin

Nathaniel Bishop. Portrait in the Bishop Memorial Library, Toms River. *Courtesy of the Bishop Memorial Library.*

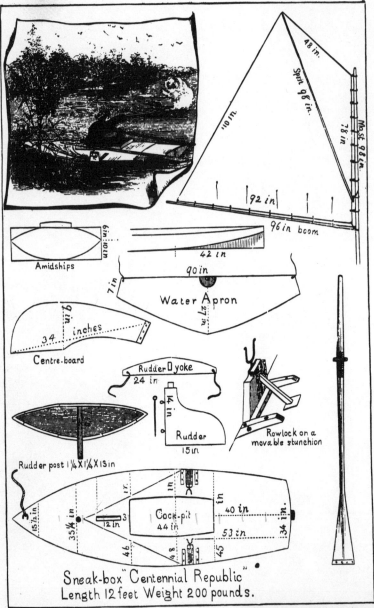

Sneak-box "Centennial Republic"
Length 12 feet Weight 200 pounds.

A 20-foot power sneakbox for fishing, built by J. H. Perrine about 1925, using the forms of the 20-foot sailing sneakbox. It was powered by a small inboard engine, had a small deck house, and of course never sailed.

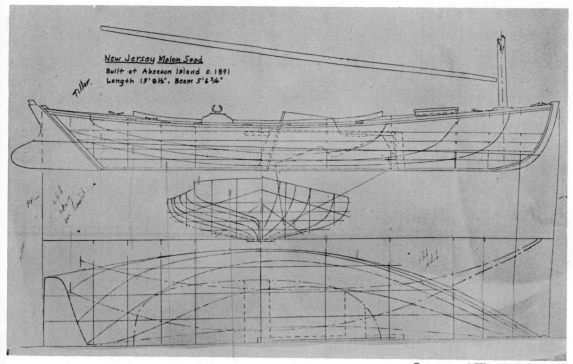

Courtesy of Wayne P. Yarnall.

MELONSEED HALF HULL

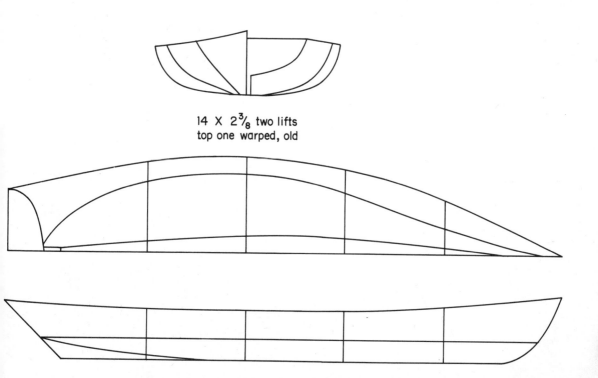

14 X 2⅜ two lifts
top one warped, old

2

The Sneakbox as Gunning Skiff

The two earliest examples of sneakbox gunning skiffs of which we have accurate sketches are one depicted by Robert B. White of Shrewsbury in *Forest and Stream,* dated April 3, 1874, and Bishop's *Centennial Republic* in 1875. The former is reproduced in this chapter and the latter in the previous chapter. The two are nearly identical in size and design. However the dagger board in White's design is about 10 inches off center, passing at the edge of the cockpit. Bishop's skiff has a centerline dagger board just forward of the cockpit. Both centerboard locations continued to be employed for many years, each having obvious advantages and shortcomings.

The centerboard well, forward of the cockpit, permitted width while the lateral location permitted length. The weight, stature, and prejudices of the gunner were served by one or the other, sometimes both.

The sneakboxes were steered by a low, long rudder on a vertical or very slightly raked transom. The rudder was controlled by lanyards, through fairleads, to a yoke or "cross rudder." The rudder lanyards passed through or over the after end of the cockpit coaming. Formerly, native gunners steered with an oar held casually against the lee rail near the stern. Occasionally, a professional gunner constructed a sneakbox without rudder or centerboard. Instead, he used a single lee (or weather) board and steered with an oar.

The publication of *Four Months in a Sneak-Box* promoted wide interest and the craft was copied by boat builders outside New Jersey for the first time.

J. Henry Rushton of Canton, New York, an outstanding canoe builder, offered a "Barnegat Sneak Boat" for duck hunting about 1881 and subsequently. The advertisement cites Bishop's *Centennial Republic* as the source of the model. The boat offered by Rushton had a deck constructed of Spanish cedar, widely used in canoe construction and the manufacture of cigar boxes. The cockpit cover was made in three sections. The weight was 175 pounds and the price $100. The advertisement contains a letter extolling its virtues from the Honorable Nicholas Longworth of Cincinnati, later Speaker of the House of Representatives. He had used one in duck hunting, finding it the best boat ever for that purpose. Rushton also offered a larger 14-foot sneakbox for two persons at $120.

Rushton's nearby competitor, The Watertown Boat and Canoe Company of Watertown, New York, offered at about the same time "the Barnegat Sneak Boat," without reference to Bishop's sneakbox or to Rushton. The boat was identical in size but was planked with white pine rather than cedar. The boat had a "radix" centerboard, of folding fan-like design. The highly competitive price was $100. A larger 14-foot boat was $120 and a still larger 16-footer cost $135.

Three other innovations were introduced in a January 8, 1885, *Forest and Stream* article. These were the use of steamed oak for frames, a centerboard rather than dagger board, and a curved rather than flat deck sheer. The curved sheer was a great advantage sailing in a steep chop or head seas in which the straight sheer designs tend to dive. Also noted is the beginning of V-shape forward sections, composed of intersecting arcs.

There were many professional, and even more numerous occasional, builders of sneakboxes. Among the recognized builders of gunning sneakboxes in the latter 19th and early 20th centuries were the following: George Bogert of Manahawkin, Bartine Clayton of Silverton, M. M. Cranmer of Cedar Run, Richard Cranmer of Manahawkin, John A. Dorsett of Point Pleasant, Shem B. Pearce of Brielle, Esek Gant of Metedeconk, Andrew Kilpatrick of Barnegat, Gus Parker of Beach Haven and Parkertown, Samuel Perrine of Barnegat, A. R. and J. W. Pharo of Tuckerton, A. Pharo of West Creek, Joel Rulon of Barnegat, Hazelton Seaman of West Creek, Joseph Truex of Metedeconk, George R. Van Sant of Atlantic City, and Jacob Vaughn of Forked River. Many of this generation were colorful personalities and highly individualistic. Their relations were highly subjective, uninfluenced by status or money. Conversely, they were well informed but not much moved by things extraneous to friends, Bay, family, and fish and game. This attitude may be misinterpreted by outlanders, particularly if self-important. A letter in *Forest and Stream* in 1885 refers to some builders as not reliable and not working steadily at their trade. The writer further complains that they consider every day spent at hard work on land as lost time and every day spent in gunning, fishing, etc., as a means of grace. These sentiments strike a responsive chord in many of us, Bayman or not. No one should be critical unless he has whiled away a warm clear spring afternoon on the marshes adjacent to the Bay.

The method of construction of the sneakbox merits a brief description. The keel is a tapered plank of the same thickness as the remainder of the bottom planking. It is called the "set-up plank" as it is the starting point of construction. It is curved to the desired profile and maintained in that form by temporarily securing it in a jig or form. The transom and sawn or bent frames are secured to the set-up plank at the proper sites. A curved horizontal member, about a third the length of the hull, and corresponding to the line of junction of bottom and deck, is secured to the forward end of the set-up plank and the ends of the forward frames. This member is a "harping" or "harpin." The bottom planking is started at the keel. Each is slightly tapered toward the ends, the inboard side being straight and the outboard side curved. Each is fastened to the transom, each frame, and the harping. Fastenings are variously screws, nails, rivets, or a combination. All planks are roughly parallel with the hull centerline and not with the waterline.

The deck planking, of tongue-and-groove cedar or pine, is fastened over the deeply curved deck frames, from transom to harping. The deck and bottom are beveled or feathered where they meet, forming an acute angle. The short deck frames at the side of the cockpit are supported alternately by stanchions or "stiffers." The cockpit floor is ceiled with light cedar fastened to the frames. The ceiling is carried to within six inches of the deck. Stops are fastened between frames at this level to prevent entrance of water. In recent years, the cockpit decking has been replaced with removable slats. In a typical 12-foot gunning skiff average scantlings are, frames $5/8$ by $7/8$ on 12-inch centers, planking $5/8$ by 5, decking $3/8$ by 4, transom $3/4$, carlins $5/8$ by $3/4$, coamings $5/8$ by 2, cockpit ceiling $3/8$ by 2, and deck frames $7/8$ by $7/8$.

There were, until very recent years, a large number of surviving gunning sneakboxes, many appearing to be from fifty to seventy years of age. These older boats were of excellent construction but were universally without builders' names. All had rectangular cockpits, folding oarlocks, washboards aft, canvas spray screen forward and an unstayed mast for spritsail or gaff rig. Any sneakbox with rounded cockpit, stayed mast, or rigged for main and jib, was probably not a gunning skiff.

Several models designed for open or rough water use have been encountered. They are longer, deeper, have a curved sheer, and V-shaped sections forward. All examples were quite old. The lines of one example, very well built, with internal racks for shells, guns and other gear, is shown. Daggerboard, spars, and rudder were missing, replaced by an outboard motor.

In recent years sneakbox gunning skiffs have been built by Carl Adams of Nacote Creek, Gus Hinrichs of New Gretna, Reuben Corlies of Manahawkin, and Allan Chadwick of Barnegat. The last named, who learned his skills working for J. H. Perrine, constructs a fine gunning skiff nearly identical with those of the 1875 era. A recent innovation has been the adaptation of fiberglass to sneakbox construction. A near classical sneakbox of fiberglass, for outboard power, is built by Re-Beck Sailboats of Perth Amboy.

In recent years, very few of these gunning craft have been built due to encroachment upon tidelands and shore pollution.

SOURCES
Publication

Forest and Stream Magazine.

Personal Reminiscences and Anecdotal Material

F. Slade Dale, Bay Head
Allan Chadwick, Barnegat
Walter Potter, Manasquan
Reuben Corlies, Manahawkin
Harry Van Sant, Atlantic City
Ronald M. Hoffman, St. Lawrence University, Canton, New York
John L. Lockhead, The Mariners Museum, Newport News, Virginia

SHREWSBURY, April 3, 1874.

EDITOR FOREST AND STREAM:—

Agreeable to promise I send you a description of a Barnegat duck boat, or, as it is called, a sneak box. This boat needs no recommendation. It has stood the test for years. Yours truly,   ROBERT B. WHITE.

Length, 12 feet. Width midships, 4 feet; width of stern, 2 feet 9 in. Depth of stern, 7 in. Sprung timbers all of one pattern, 9-16x13-16 in. distance apart, 8 in. deck timbers natural bend, 1 in.x¼ in Cock-pit, inside measurement, length 3 feet 4 in. width at bow and stern, 18¼ in. midships, 19 in. Combing, height of inside at bow and stern, 2¼ in., midships, 2 in. From bottom of combing to top ceiling, 13 in. Trunk on port side, set slanting to take a 15 in. board trunk placed alongside and abaft of forward corner of combing. Rowlocks, height 6 in. from coaming 9 in. middle of to stern, 4 feet 7 in., made to fold down inboard and to fasten up with a hook. Stool rack runs from rowlocks to stern, notched at ends into fastenings of rowlocks, also notched at corners and hooked together, rest against a cleat on deck outside, and are hooked to the deck inside. In a heavy sea the apron is used. It is held up by a stick from peak to combing. Thus rigged the boat has the reputation of being able to live as long as oars can be pulled. The apron is tacked to the deck about tow-thirds its length. The wings are fastened to the top and bottom of the rowlocks. Mast hole 2⅛ in., 2 in. from coaming. Drop of sides from top of deck, 5¼ in., dead rise, 8 in. Over cock-pit a hatch is placed. Everything connected with the boat is placed inside, gunners, often leaving their guns, &c., locking the hatch fast. The boats sail well and covered with sedge are used to shoot from. With the hatch on a person can be protected from rain, and with blankets, can be accommodated with a night's lodging. With this I send a working model: scale 1 inch to the foot. The "Fishing Tourist" I find very interesting. We have no fishing, thanks to our laws that give us no protection from eel and other seines. Our legislators don't take the FOREST AND STREAM.

P. S.—Boards for boats, white cedar, ⅝ in thick, deck narrow strips tongued and grooved.   R. B. W.

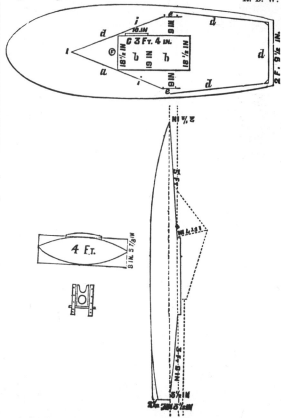

a a—Apron. 1 1 1 shows where it is nailed to deck.
b b—Cock-pit.
c—Trunk.
d d d—Stool rack.
e e—Rowlocks.
Fig. 4 shows rowlocks.

Description and plan of a sneakbox, published in *Forest and Stream*, 1874.

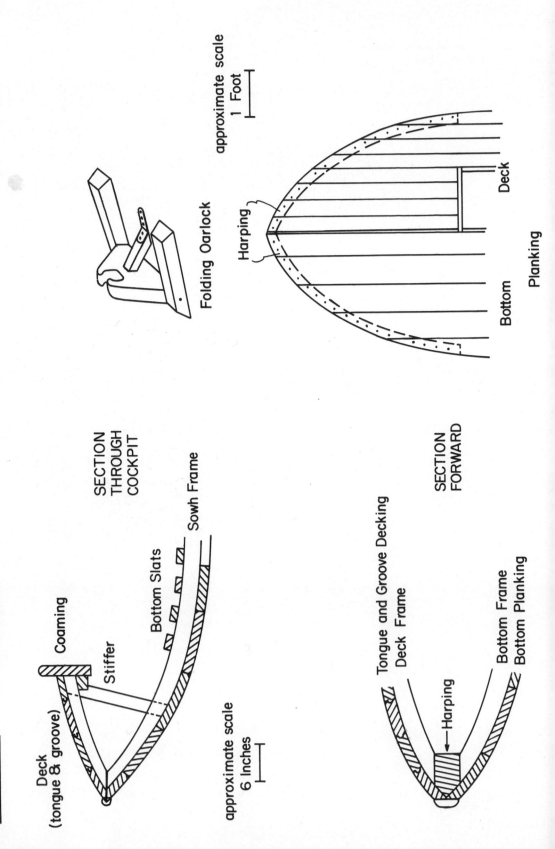

SNEAK BOX— construction details

Deck (tongue & groove)

Coaming

Stiffer

Bottom Slats

Sowh Frame

SECTION THROUGH COCKPIT

approximate scale 6 Inches

Folding Oarlock

Harping

Deck

Bottom

Planking

approximate scale 1 Foot

Tongue and Groove Decking

Deck Frame

Harping

Bottom Frame

Bottom Planking

SECTION FORWARD

The Barnegat Sneak Boat.

Length 12 feet, greatest width 4 feet; width of stern 34 inches; depth of stern 7 inches, depth amidship 16 inches. This boat built by our smooth method, is particularly adapted to hunting and fishing as it will float on very shallow water, is a good sailer and a dry boat.

We build this boat of $\frac{3}{8}$ inch pine planking put together our smooth method, ribbed with oak, stern and keelson all of oak; oak pieces $\frac{3}{4}$x$\frac{1}{8}$ lengthwise on each side of keelson 5 inches from keelson. This stiffens and protects the boat.

Deck two colors of hardwood. Hatches made lighter, in sections, to lock up. Cockpit 7 feet by 20 inches, pointed flaring coaming of hardwood copper and brass fastened; hull painted, deck finished in natural wood, oiled and varnished. Fitted out with Radix center board, one pair oars, rudder, outriggers, cleats and ring, all brass, nickel plated. 3-inch mast tube with plate.

Price on above described $98 00

Purchaser can select sail he wishes to use and add price as found in list. This boat is built in three sizes 14 and 16 feet long.

No. 2. Built and finished same as No. 1, only of greater capacity and more roomy. Price $110.00.

No. 3. Same as No. 2, only of still greater capacity. Price $135.00

Mariners Museum
I. 1885   *Watertown Boat and Canoe Co.*

The sneakbox was adopted by a number of builders, far from its home waters. *Courtesy of the Mariners' Museum, Newport News, Va.*

THE BARNEGAT SNEAK BOAT.
No. 1.

Mr. N. H. Bishop's "Centennial Republic," from which I was kindly permitted to take the model, weighed about two hundred pounds, yet owing to its spoon shaped bottom the hunter is able to drag it over marsh or beach and use it among ice where a light canoe would soon be ruined. By thatching the deck with grass or bushes it is used for a *blind* (and for that reason sometimes called a Sneak *Box*) and as such, can be used on the shore among the reeds and rushes, or anchored on the water equally well. At the end of the day's hunt the sportsman can gather in his game and decoys, hoist his sail and hie away across bay or lake to hotel or home, or if it be too rough for sailing, draw hatch and apron close around him and start a spruce breeze of his own. In the latter case it is said she can live in *any sea* as long as oars can be pulled.

DIMENSIONS—Length, 12 ft.; greatest width, 4 ft.; width of stern, 34 inches; depth of stern, 7 inches; greatest depth amidships, 16 inches.

MATERIAL—Timbers *white cedar* sawed ¾x1½ inch, placed 5¼ inches apart; stern and skag of oak, also two pieces of oak on the bottom ¾x⅞ inches, 6 inches apart, lengthwise of the boat to protect the bottom in drawing it on the ground.

PLANKING— *White cedar* ⅜ inch thick (9 streaks) put on "ship lap."

DECK AND HATCHES—⅜ Spanish Cedar.

COCK-PIT—About 20x72 inchs, (can be made any other size without extra cost) with a combing of hard wood 1¼ inches high. This is covered with a hatch in three sections with staples, hasp and padlock so that everything can be locked up inside of the boat for transportation.

Her fittings are a rudder, a pair of brass rowlocks standing 8½ inches above deck and made to fold inboard upon the deck when not in use, a pair of spruce oars, centerboard, mast and sail. She is copper fastened and finished in oil and varnish, a first-class boat throughout—will weigh complete about 175 lbs.

Price Complete, $100.

Hon. Nicholas Longworth, of Cincinnati, ex-Commodore of the A. C. A., in speaking of this boat says: "The Sneak Boat is a complete success. I have shot a great many ducks out of it this spring. It is by far the best boat for this purpose that I have ever seen and under sail handles as well as a cat boat.

Mariner Museum — C. 188?

SNEAK BOAT.
No. 2.

Like No. 1, except that it is 14 feet long and with cock-pit 8 feet long, for two persons.

Price Complete, $120.00.

The sails best suited for this boat are Nos. 13 or 15. *Built only to order.* Time required, four to six weeks.

These boats are built coarse and cheap by other builders. The sportsman who wants them for hard usage only, can, perhaps, do better than to buy of us, but if he wants a fine sailer, *very safe*, to take ladies or children out in—a fine boat in every way, yet one that he can use to advantage for hunting when wanted, let him come to us.

The Nessmuk Canoes.
Nos. 161 and 162.

These canoes are probably the *lightest* ones ever made for actual use. They are built of $\frac{3}{16}$ cedar, ribbed 1½ inches apart, without seats or thwarts, will be finished in oil and varnish, or painted, as preferred, and furnished with one double bladed paddle. Built only to order.

Of her Mr. Geo. W. Sears—"Nessmuk" in *Forrest and Stream*—says: "You ask what of the little canoe? and say you think she is too small." "I don't know; she was large enough to carry me (110) and forty pounds of duffle on all the Fulton lakes, on the Moose, on Blue Mountain lake, on Raquette, Eagle—anywhere I wanted to go. Too small for handling a *very* large salmon, or an open contest with a deer on the lakes perhaps, and not as comfortable as a larger, broader boat. But for a cedar boat of 18 *pounds* or less, she was, and is, a marvel of steadiness; and she is *tight and staunch yet*, after being paddled over 550 *miles* on lakes, rivers, outlets, inlets, creeks, &c., and jumping her over rocks in the rapids that might have wrecked a heavier boat."

We do not publish this statement to persuade any one that they had better buy an *eighteen pound* canoe, for very few men would like one so small, but rather to show that if *such* a boat without being *strengthened by seats, thwarts or braces* will carry 150 pounds *tight and tight* after a $50 *mile cruise*, the purchaser of the larger sizes has nothing to fear for their strength or seaworthiness.

Watertight compartments can be made in the ends of any of these boats or canoes by putting in bulk-heads and decking over the part (usually about 3 ft.) toward the ends. The *extra* cost for this is from six to ten dollars per boat, according to size and the length of the compartment. It can only be done with boats *built to order* as it cannot be added after the boat is completed.

The Barnegat Sneak Boat

For duck hunting, is by many thought to be the best in the world. Certainly it possesses some characteristics not found in any other craft. Its peculiar model (which first gave it the nickname "Devil's Coffin") has some advantages not found in any other. It is not a light boat.

Mr. N. H. Bishop's "Centennial Republic," from which I was kindly permitted to take the model, weighed about two hundred pounds, yet owing to its spoon shaped bottom the hunter is able to drag it over marsh or beach and use it among ice where a light canoe would soon be ruined. By thatching the deck with grass or bushes it is used for a *blind* (and for that reason sometimes called a *Sneak Box*) and as such, can be used on the shore among the reeds and rushes, or anchored on the water equally well. At the end of the day's hunt the sportsman can gather in his game and decoys, hoist his sail and hie away across bay or lake to hotel or home, or if it be too rough for sailing draw hatch and apron close around him and start a spruce breeze of his own. In which ease it is said she can live in *any sea* as long as oars can be pulled.

While keeping the model and material intact, I have made such little changes in the make up as experience in making light boats suggested would be best, the most important of which is *lighter* timbers and twice as many of them, enabling me to use a trifle lighter planking and decks. The former I have thought best to "ship lap" instead of "jointing and calking."

For a much more minute description than can be given in a limited space of a builder's catalogue see "Four Months in a Sneak Box," written by N. H. Bishop (ex-Secretary of the American Canoe Association, P. O. address, Lake George, Warren Co., N. Y.) and published by Lee & Shepard, of Boston.

The little craft carried the author safely 2600 miles amid the ice packs of the Ohio, the snags and bars of the Mississippi, and the coral reefs and coon oyster beds on the coast of the gulf of Mexico.

DIMENSIONS—Length 12 ft.; greatest width 4 ft.; width of stern 34 inches; depth of stern 7 inches; greatest depth amidships 16 inches.

MATERIAL—Timbers *white cedar* sawed ¾ × 1½ inch, placed 5½ inches apart; stem and skag or keel of oak, also two pieces of oak on the bottom ¾ × ⅞ inches, 6 inches apart, lengthwise of the boat to protect bottom in drawing it on the ground.

PLANKING—*White cedar* ⅜ inch thick (9 streaks) put on "ship lap."

DECK—⅜ white cedar matched together.

COCK-PIT—About 20×72 inches, (can be made any other size without extra cost) with a combing of red elm 1¼ inches high. This is covered with a hatch in three sections with staples, hasp and padlock so that everything can be locked up inside of the boat for transportation.

Her fittings are a rudder, a pair of brass rowlocks standing 8¼ inches above deck and made to fold inboard onto the deck, when

No. 175.

not in use, a pair of spruce oars, centre-board, mast and sail. She is copper fastened and well painted and finished, a first-class boat throughout—will weigh complete about 175 lbs.

Price Complete, $85.

Hon. Nicholas Longworth, of Cincinnati, Commodore of the A. C. A., in speaking of this boat says: "The Sneak Boat is a complete success. I have shot a great many ducks out of it this spring It is by far the best boat for this purpose that I have ever seen and under sail handles as well as a cat boat."

No. 176.

Is like No. 175 only a cheaper made boat. Her planking and deck are of cedar. Timbers 1 x 1¼ inches placed 11 inches apart with a stout elm rib (bent) between, fastened with tinned iron nails, malleable iron rowlocks and galvanized iron trimmings instead of brass. A good durable boat.

Price Complete, $75.

No. 177.

Like No. 175 except that it is 14 feet long and with cock-pit 8 feet long for two persons.

Price Complete, $100.

No. 178.

In size like No. 177; in material and make up like No. 176. We do not always have these boats in stock and usually require two or three weeks time in which to fill an order

Price Complete, $90.

Flat Bottom Duck Boat.

No. 180.

Weight complete about 80 pounds; price $15; length 14 feet; width on bottom 28 inches; on top 38 inches; depth amidships 11 inches; at ends 15 inches; sharp at both ends; stems and knees natural crooks, the former oak, the latter spruce; siding ⅜ inch cedar 3 streaks on each side; bottom ½ inch cedar matched together; sides and bottom are both attached to a corner piece of oak or elm thus making a very stout boat; has two seats; is copper fastened and well painted; fitted with one pair brass row locks, one pair of oars and one maple paddle; well liked by those who have used them; built to order only.

CANOEING AND CANOES.

We do not think at this late day we need say much in the abstract of canoeing. Far abler pens than ours have already written upon the subject until even "he who runs may read."

Nearly all know of the rapid strides toward popularity made during the past half dozen years, especially in the United States, by this innocent and health giving sport. Then, there was, we believe but a single canoe club (The N. Y. C. C.,) in the country, and the few canoes owned were either built by amateurs or had been imported from England, the country that gave birth to the sport. To-day there are scores of canoe clubs having a membership of several hundred. The American Canoe Association with its two hundred and fifty members, besides hundreds of enthusiastic canoeists who belong to no organization, but whose sails have caught the breeze on hundreds of the lakes, bays and rivers, with which OUR COUNTRY to a greater extent than any other is blest.

But after all canoeing is but in its infancy here, and we have many things to learn from the pen of a Bishop or an Alden, or from what is better still, our own personal experience.

To us, as builders, belongs the duty—a duty not unmixed with pleasure—of providing the canoeist with a suitable craft wherewith to explore the many devious and beautiful water courses intersecting our broad land.

The "copy" in our writing book when we were a boy, "many men of many minds" applies with considerable force to many men intent upon the purchase of a canoe. So long as that remains a fact, it will be impossible—even if it were desirable—to have any one model, any one mode of construction or any one builder please all.

It depends very much upon the individual canoeist as well as the waters upon which he will use his canoe, as to what model will suit him best. If for streams, for inland cruising where the paddle is used as much as the sail, and when carries are frequent, no models will be found equal to *The American Traveling Canoe* or the *Stella Maris*. And while these canoes will *take* where any will, those models having greater breadth of beam, the *Shadow, Princess*, and their various modifications, are more generally preferred on open water where there are no carries and where the wind is mainly depended upon for propelling power.

BARNEGAT SNEAK-BOX

GUNNING and FISHING BOAT

12 Feet Long 4 Feet Beam

Complete as shown with Sail. Spars.
Center Board. Hatch. Oar Locks.
Storm Curtain, Cable and Decoy Rack.

PRICE - - - - $140.00

J. H. PERRINE

BARNEGAT, NEW JERSEY

The classic gunning sneakbox as built by Perrine, almost unchanged for a century. Note the price in 1935.

BARNEGAT SNEAK-BOX

15-Foot FISHING BOAT
Out Board Motor Model

$300.00

Price with Hood. -

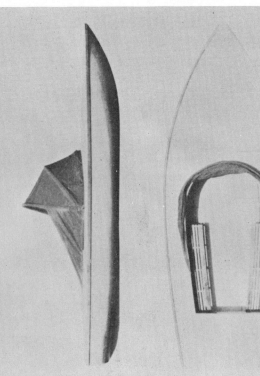

Designed and Built by

J. H. PERRINE NEW JERSEY

BARNEGAT, NEW JERSEY

A variation on the gunning sneakbox. This was never popular.

Contemporary gunning sneakbox, a classic 12-foot model by Chadwick, still unchanged.

Rough water sneakbox.

Sneakbox bottom. Note method of planking.

Modern gunning sneakbox and one under construction. Note set-up plank or keel, partially planked bottom, transom, frames, and harping.

RE—BECK SAILBOATS

332 PROSPECT STREET   PERTH AMBOY, N. J.   08861

TEL. 826-9237

"ALL FIBERGLASS BARNEGAT SNEAK BOX DUCK BOAT KIT"

"OUTSTANDING FEATURES"

Unsinkable — Foam Flotation
Molded Fiberglass Hull — Hull and Deck are of Trouble Free Molded
    Fiberglass for Lowest Maintenance, Lightest Weight, Greatest Durability and best
    Appearance.
Colors Molded in — Fiberglass Hull and Deck are Supplied with Colors
    Permantely Molded in for Lasting Beauty with Little Maintenance
Portable — Easily Transported on top of Car
Solid Mahogany Oar Locks - and Motor Mount
Low Silhouette and Shallow Draft
Rot Proof, Leak Proof, Waterproof, will not soak up water.
Skeg and Bottom Runners Molded in for Extra Structural Strength.

THE BARNEGAT SNEAK BOX

The Barnegat Sneak Box is one of the oldest and most famous small boats being built in New Jersey. It got its start over one hundred years ago. Most of the original builders have long since gone leaving the building of these famous boats to their successors.

The Sneak Box is used by Duck Hunters because it is actually a floating propelled duck blind since it is camoflaged by being painted with. A dull dead grass color. It has a shallow draft for entering very shallow water and can be beached rapidly. It is a very seaworthy boat and can take severe punishment. Also, it is one of the safest boats afloat having a very wide beam giving it much stability.

These boats were originally all built out of well seasoned Jersey Cedar. However, with the trend going tremendously in favor of fiberglass boats several builders are now making fiberglass Barnegat Sneak Boxes both as Duck Boats and also as Sailing Models.

The advantage of being built out of fiberglass is that they are much lighter and makes trailering unnecessary, since the boat is light enough for car toppong. No caulking is necessary and the boat is ready to use at all times. It will not leak or rot and will last many years.

The Barnegat Sneak Box also makes an excellent fishing skiff due to its wide beam, stability, and car top lightness. It can be rowed, sailed, or powered by a light outboard motor.

"Re-becks" all fiberglass Barnegat Sneak Box

"IDEAL CAR TOPPER"

KIT PRICE

$295.00

"KIT - PRICE INCLUDES"

One piece fiberglass deck
One piece fiberglass hull
All wood parts - frames, carlins, gussets, floor
    board, motor mount, oar locks and mounting
    blocks, ring bolt, fiberglass mat and resin
    for bonding frames to hull, all necessary
    screws, nuts, bolts, full set of instructions
    and schematics.

"SPECIFICATIONS"

Length — 12 Ft.
Beam — 52 Inches
Weight — 130 Lbs. Approx.
Color   — Dead Grass
Recommended Motor - 3 to 5 H. P.

"ACCESSORIES"

Canvas Spray Shield	$12.00
Decoy Racks	8.00

ALL PRICES F. O. B. PERTH AMBOY, N. J.

Although now built of fiberglass, it is still a sneakbox.

3

The Racing Sneakboxes

The early sneakboxes proved excellent sailers and their competitive possibilities were soon recognized.

Racing was largely impromptu, the principal Barnegat Bay competition being between the larger catboats centered in the area of Beach Haven and Toms River. Nathaniel Bishop continued to influence the increase in sneakbox popularity, as the author, or encourager of other authors, of articles in sporting magazines. A 16-foot sneakbox for pleasure sailing only was designed by J. Kilpatrick of Barnegat and its lines were published in *Forest and Stream*, January 8, 1885. The cockpit of this handsome sneakbox was large enough for three or four persons. The advanced features of its design were indicated in a previous chapter. The rig was a balanced lug, a type borrowed from the sailing canoe. About 1890 an 18-foot gaff-rigged sneakbox became popular, was raced on the Bay and grew to a fleet of about thirty.

The success of the local sneakboxes and increasing local interest attracted the talents of naval architects, including that of E. B. Schock. The design of Schock's modernized 17-foot sneakbox was printed in the November 22, 1902, *Forest and Stream*. Schock had increased the freeboard, further curved the sheer, filled out the bilges and rounded the bow to a shape approaching that of the later inland lake scows. The overall dimensions were: length 17 ft.; beam 6 ft. 6 in.; mast 21 ft.; boom 19 ft.; and gaff 12 ft. 3 in. The sail area was approximately 450 sq. ft. The number and popularity of this design is unknown. Planking wide shallow hulls of this type presented many difficulties and resulted in some very tortured planks. Occasionally the complex and difficult shape at the extreme forward end was attained by using a large block of cedar, contoured to proper shape, into which the ends of the planking were rabbeted. The rounded, scow-like bows of these and other later similar designs were considered by the Baymen as inspired by the hospital bedpan.

In 1906, a new class was introduced which limited overall length to 20 feet. This limitation may partially be the result of the consistent success of one of the older 18-foot sneakboxes. The 20-foot class were gaff rigged, carrying 450 to 600 square feet of sail. They were still remembered as being wooden ships requiring iron men. These "sandbaggers" ordinarily had a crew of six, whose principal occupation was to manage the eighteen to twenty thirty-pound sandbags. In a heavy breeze the number of sandbags increased to thirty or thirty-five and crew to eight. Going about in a 20-knot breeze called for care, good judgment and stamina on the part of the crew. From 8 to 12 seconds was required to shift the ballast bags. A gybe in a fresh breeze was a rare adventure, occasionally accompanied by a broken mast. Running was a barely balanced complex of contradictory forces, especially in a sea. With a sea under the stern, the hulls buried their bows, requiring a surge aft of all hands. When the sea had run under to the bow, there was a sickening deceleration which prompted all hands forward. The lateral balance was poor so that a broad reach in a fresh breeze often required two men on the tiller to control the barn door rudder. By 1910 about fifty of these boats had been built, largely by Morton Johnson of Bay Head. Most skippers had difficulty in obtaining a crew, except by impressment. On the dock, the skippers were always recognizable by their large biceps and stern visages. These monumental craft, with a 6-inch-diameter mast, heavy galvanized shrouds and forestay, stern boomkin for the multisheeved main sheet, and boom extending 6 feet beyond the transom are still remembered sixty years later.

In 1914, a new class of 16-footers was introduced. This was designed by C. D. Mower to do away with the major design weaknesses of the 20-footers. The new sneakbox was lighter, had a rounder, fuller, more scow-like bow and a smaller rig. They were nearly flat-bottomed, well-balanced, had full bilges, no skegs, and a small deep rudder. Their introduction by members of the Island Heights and Seaside Park Yacht Clubs resulted in humiliating defeat of the older, builder-designed class. The gaff rig was replaced by a Marconi rig in 1924. The new rig promptly outclassed the performance of the previous boats. Their reputation as the fastest boats on the Bay was ended in turn by the introduction of the 28-foot class E bilge-board scows from the Great Lakes about 1925.

The sneakbox, however, was not done for. A new, smaller, cheaper sneakbox, 15 feet in length, was designed by J. H. Perrine of Barnegat about 1918. It was introduced sometime before 1920, when the Polyhue Yacht Club of Beachwood purchased a fleet of seven. The popularity of the 15-footer was overwhelming, spreading rapidly to other clubs. It had come at the right time, filling a postwar need. The design achieved respectability and further recognition when officially designated as a class by the Barnegat Bay Yacht Racing Association. By 1927, 400 had been built by Perrine. Eventually, about 3,000 were built and widely disseminated. Perrine, the original and "official" builder dominated the scene for many years. An exception was a group of twenty-five built by Eli Townsend of Seaside Park for the Seaside Park Yacht Club.

Perrine's shop in Barnegat was a center of great activity. He was able to attract a large number of skilled, and previously independent, boat builders, who were paid on a piecework basis. Excellent organization by Perrine and a basically good design permitted rapid but excellent construction. Many semifinished hulls were moved from Perrine's to the shops of other local builders for completion. The 15-foot class underwent eventual modifications in rig and in class organization. However, many thirty- and forty-year-old hulls of the original design survived. A few later examples were provided with two mast steps permitting the use of either a sloop or catboat rig. Other later builders were Morton Johnson and Zack Johnson of Bay Head, David Beaton of West Mantoloking, and probably others.

The 15-foot sneakbox was inexpensive, costing between $225 and $250. It provided a safe training class for many generations of junior and senior sailors down to the present time. It was one of the largest class of one-design boats ever developed. They continue in use to the present time.

Other less numerous classes of sneakboxes were built. One, a 14-footer of conventional proportions, was designed by Allan Chadwick in 1960. This, called the "8 Ball," was an excellent performer. Chadwick also introduced at various times a newer modified 15½-footer and an 18-footer.

Smaller, 12-foot junior sailers were introduced using sneakbox design, including the "Butterfly" class by Perrine. The "Diamond" class, used by the Island Heights Yacht Club and the same size sneakbox designed by Phillip Clark are examples. The former was built by Perrine, Beaton, and Fitzpatrick, the latter only by Beaton. Boats of the latter class are still used by the Bay Head, Mantoloking, and Manasquan River Yacht Clubs.

A small number of other classes and various sized sneakboxes have been constructed. Farragut Academy, on Toms River, used a group of 18-foot Marconi rigged sneakboxes built by Chadwick. A larger 24-foot class had been introduced but never proceeded beyond the prototype stage. Their introduction coincided with that of the vastly superior inland lake scows.

A few other recognized builders of sneakboxes merit inclusion. William Bowker of Barnegat was employed in the Perrine shop. He also constructed excellent sneakboxes on his own account. Benjamin Hance of Point Pleasant constructed small numbers of class sneakboxes to about 1925. Henry and Washington Peterson of Barnegat had been employed in the Perrine shop and continued to build sneakboxes on their own account. Henry Kilpatrick of Barnegat built a variety of small boats including sneakboxes.

The employment and development of the sneakbox as a limited cruiser merits mention. It was initially explored in the January 8, 1885, *Forest and Stream*. An article described a 14-foot sneakbox built by George Bogert of Manahawkin, constructed for a member of the "Singlehand Cruising Club." This featured a separate small hatch in the after deck covering a small galley with a coal oil stove. The price of this capsule cruiser was $85. Some of the later 24-foot sneakboxes, built in the mid-1920's, were adopted for limited cruising by various expedients.

It does not seem right to leave the waters of Barnegat Bay without a final passing word about its people, the unusual breed known as Baymen. The term incidentally is only used in its masculine gender, there being no Baywomen. This does not imply that the Baymen were celibate. They were universally married and almost universally sired large families. The waters of the Bay start properly at Bay Head and extend southward through the adjacent counties. The Bay influence extends north a few miles to include the waters of the Manasquan River. The earlier inhabitants shared the characteristics of those farther south who made their living on or by the waters and shores or who became Baymen by inunction, interest, or sympathy.

SOURCES

Publications

Forest and Stream Magazine.
Sailing Craft, by Edwin J. Schoettle.

Personal Reminiscences and Anecdotal Material

S. Slade Dale, Bay Head
Allan Chadwick, Barnegat
David Beaton, West Mantoloking
Mrs. Harry H. Kroh, Brielle

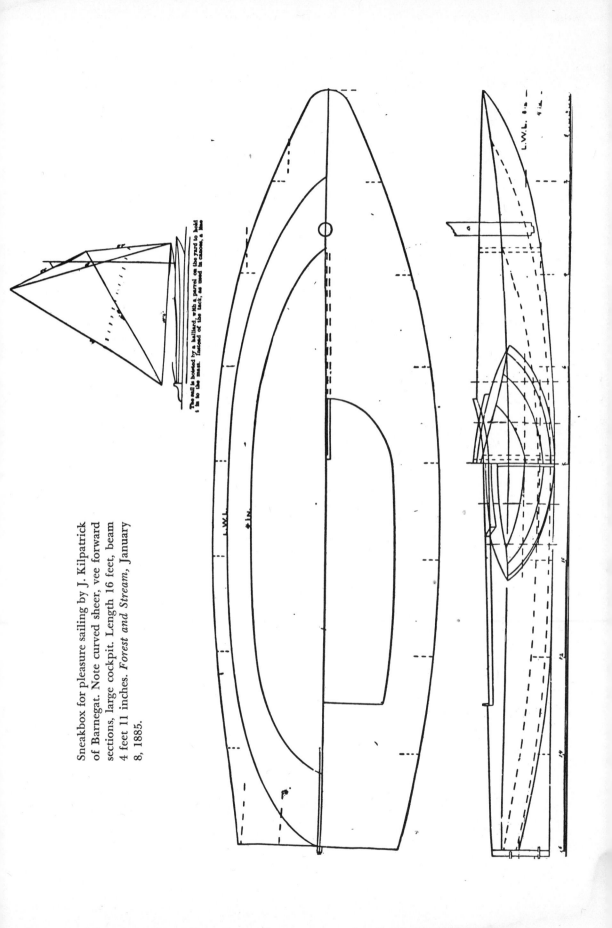

Sneakbox for pleasure sailing by J. Kilpatrick of Barnegat. Note curved sheer, vee forward sections, large cockpit. Length 16 feet, beam 4 feet 11 inches. *Forest and Stream*, January 8, 1885.

BARNEGAT SNEAK-BOX

BUTTERFLY TYPE

12 Feet Long   5 Feet Beam

COMPLETE AS SHOWN

Price   -   -   -   - $200.00

J. H. PERRINE

BARNEGAT,   NEW JERSEY

One of the earlier sailing types which preceded the popular 15-footer.

Fifteen-foot Perrine sneakboxes awaiting delivery in Barnegat Bay about 1925.

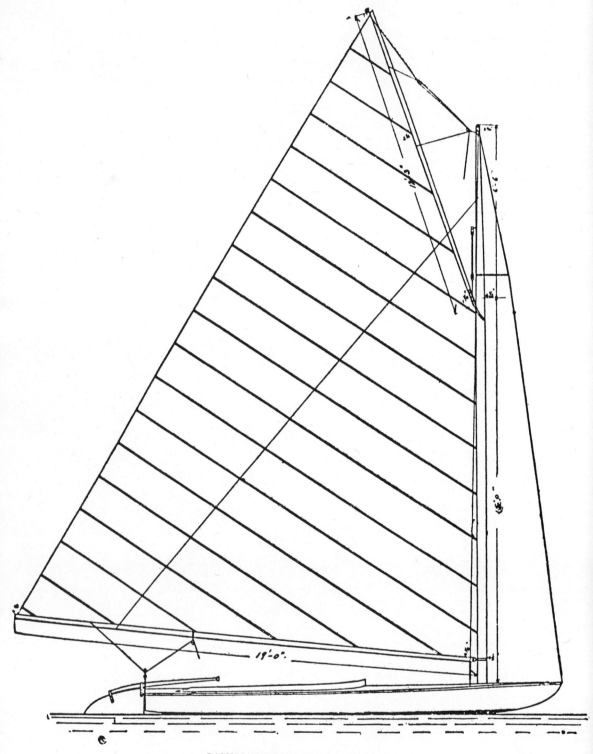

BARNEGAT SNEAK-BOX—SAIL PLAN.
Designed by E. B. Schock.

From *Forest and Stream*, November 22, 1902.

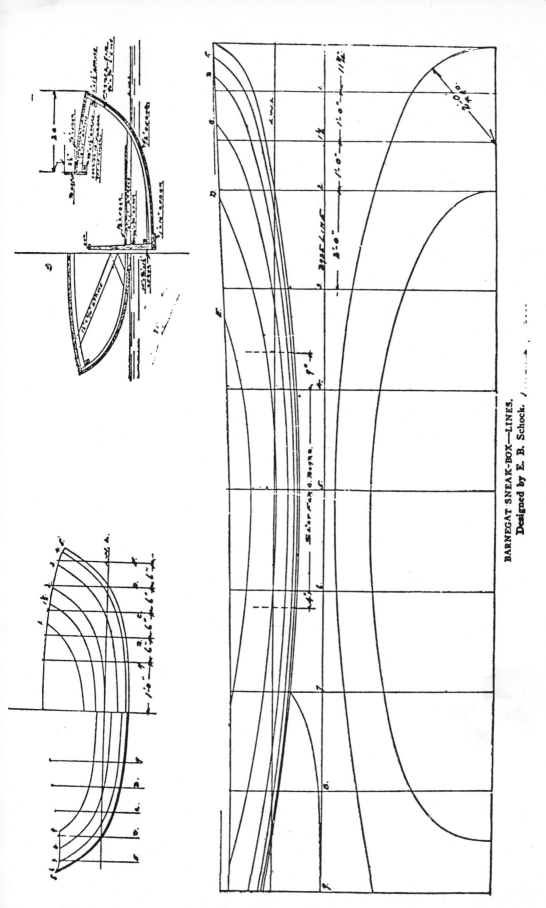

BARNEGAT SNEAK-BOX—LINES.
Designed by E. B. Schock. ————, - - - - -

The hull of this sneakbox anticipates the later popular scow form. From *Forest and Stream*, November 22, 1902.

Contemporary 16-foot sloop-rigged sneakbox by Chadwick, 1942.

4

Rail Gunning Skiffs

Gunning skiffs discussed in other chapters are the Barnegat Bay sneak-box, the melonseed and other less common craft.

Another specialized type known as rail gunning skiffs, reed bird skiffs, push skiffs or pole boats were slender double-enders, some of which were equipped for working under sail. They were developed for hunting rail and other waterfowl in the creeks, marshes, sedge, and reeds bordering Delaware Bay and River and were also used in the waters of Great Egg Harbor River and occasionally elsewhere.

The principal game, the sora rail, frequents and feeds in fresh-water marshes with dense vegetation. The marshes are passable for the skiffs only at high water. Hunting can start one or one and a half hours before flood and lasts a like time after. The skiff is propelled in the reeds by poling. The poler stands on the after deck or in the after end of the cockpit, depending on relative weights of poler and gunner and the design of the skiff. The gunner stands in the fore part of the cockpit, rarely on the deck. As the boat is pushed through the reeds, the poler may aid in flushing birds by striking the reeds with his pole. The able and experienced poler calls the rise of the birds as "mark right," "mark left," etc. The rail does not fly high or fast so the range is less than twenty yards. Even so, the rail can be an elusive target. Guns range from 410 to 12 gauge, usually cylinder bored doubles. The more proficient gunners favor the smaller bore pieces. As gunning is limited to about two hours at each flood, downed birds are not immediately retrieved but their location is marked.

The rail skiffs were commonly about 16 feet long with a 4-foot beam. They strongly resemble the Adirondack guide boats but predate them. Surviving examples of four subtypes will be described separately.

The sailing gunning skiffs were much like the "Delaware ducker" described by H. I. Chappelle. Two poorly preserved and incomplete examples were used in developing a composite sketch plan. The hulls were lap-straked with seven or eight light cedar planks to a side. The heavier bottom or keel plank of cedar was protected by a light white oak shoe or battens. Planking was copper riveted, rarely cinch nailed, to light steam-bent white oak frames closely spaced. The light scantlings are indicated on the sketch. There were short fore and aft decks and usually covering boards. Earlier models had only an aft deck. The New Jersey boats appear to have been provided with a pivoted centerboard rather than a daggerboard. The lines of the ends were symmetrical and waterlines convex. Buoyancy at the ends was needed in gunning. The stern was straight for 10 to 12 inches between gudgeons and was slightly raked. The rudder was small in area and roughly circular in profile. The midsection had a small amount of deadrise from the edge of the wide plank keel. The bilge was a smooth arc to the gunwale, producing a somewhat slack bilge.

Several contemporary renderings of gunning skiffs and hunting scenes by Thomas Eakins furnish much data. Eakins' father owned property near Fairton on Cohansey Creek where father and son frequently hunted together. Eakins, luckily for our purposes, was an excellent and careful draughtsman who depicted the skiffs in much detail. *The Artist and His Father Hunting Reed Birds* was painted in 1874. Thomas is shown in the stern poling while Benjamin, his father, stands forward with gun ready. This skiff has a short after deck and is probably the same boat shown under sail in *Starting Out After Rail*, painted in 1874 and exhibited in the Boston Museum of Fine Arts. The skiff is shown under sail with a low, horizontal, spritsail rig. A similar boat and rig are shown in profile in the background. There is no foredeck and after deck is fairly short. The centerboard box, deck, rudder, tiller, rig, and push pole are shown. Eakins, and probably his father, are the passengers. A watercolor rendering of the same scene in the Wichita Art Museum is nearly identical.

Another painting, *Will Schuster and Black Man Going Shooting*, was painted in 1876. This shows a somewhat different gunning skiff with fore and aft decks and covering boards. Other paintings by Eakins, and magazine illustrations based upon them, show gunning skiffs in use hunting rail. A gunning skiff had been built for Eakins by Michael Myers, a master boat builder of Fairton. Myers annually overhauled and painted it. This is probably one of the boats depicted by Eakins.

In the late 19th century, the sailing gunning skiffs were occasionally rigged with a raking mast and triangular sail, Chesapeake bateau style. A very similar second type of skiff was found with provision for a mast and sail but without centerboard or daggerboard. Gudgeons had been previously removed. The skiff had probably employed an external fin or keel, possibly a leeboard.

The earliest known builders of gunning skiffs were Benjamin D. Sparks of Westville on Big Timber Creek, Henry Husted of Fairton, and Evan Seeds of Bridgeboro on Rancocas Creek, all prior to 1850. Another early builder was John B. Gray of Bridgeport on Racoon Creek. His name appears in an 1866 directory and in the 1870 census. The census indicates he had been born in New Jersey in 1818 and in 1870 produced nine gunning skiffs valued all together at $288, plus a considerable amount of other building. Another builder of gunning skiffs during this period was James L. Kemble of Bridgeboro. His reputation for craftsmanship was wide and he shipped skiffs over a large area of the eastern states. Other builders were William Smith of Burlington, David Mills of Fairton, Lewis Steel of Delanco, Thomas Stevens of Woodbury, Michael and Joseph M. Myers of Fairton, Claude Bateman of Mauricetown and J. S. Lamson of Bordentown. Lamson, a shipbuilder as well, had also built a wood-planked canoe used by Nathaniel H. Bishop in an inland voyage in 1876.

A third type of double-ended gunning skiff had no provision for sail. They were of the same general size, shape, and construction and were produced by the same group of builders. They were decked at the ends for 2½ to 3½ feet. In one unusual example, the foredeck was flat, secured to the underside of the sheer clamp and was provided with shallow battens. It was obviously a platform for the gunner. The skiffs had floorboards, one or two thwarts, oarlocks and often a low platform forward of the after deck. An occasional skiff is found with a long foredeck, short after deck, covering boards, elliptical cockpit and low coaming. These had low platforms at the ends of the cockpit. The skiffs which were not designed for sailing had a flatter midsection without deadrise.

The fourth group of double-ended gunning skiffs were of bateau or sharpie construction. They were of the same general dimensions and proportions but had a slightly rockered flat bottom and slightly flared flat sides. They are of more recent vintage than the preceding three types, probably starting about 1900. All were built with covering boards and decks which aided in maintaining hull shape. They are usually heavier than the preceding types weighing up to 150 pounds. Many have been recently fiberglassed by enthusiasts and are very heavy indeed.

One example, a very well-built and rugged one, has sides of one piece of white cedar, ¾ inch in thickness. The sides are 11 inches wide in the center and 13 inches at the ends. They flare 15 degrees. The bottom is planked longitudinally with the same white cedar planking 6 to 6½ inches wide. The frames are of ¾-inch cedar sided 1¼ inches on 12-inch centers which increases to 19 inches towards bow and stern. There are alternate cedar knees doubling the frames at sheer and bottom. Sheer clamp and chine are also of ¾-inch cedar. The bottom is nailed to both sides and chine. The foredeck is 42 inches and the after deck 22 inches in length. The covering boards are 4 inches wide. Deck and covering boards are of ⅝-inch cedar. There is a cockpit coaming 1½ inches high. The bottom sheer is 3 inches and that of the topsides about 5 inches. Displacement was usually calculated so as to have bow and stern just in the water, a heavier boat and crew requiring proportionally more bottom sheer. There is a low platform at the after end of the cockpit, 3 inches higher than the floor boards. There

are other similar boats, usually built with lighter scantlings. Workmanship on all examples examined was very good to excellent. Other
examples of flat-bottom design have sides which are lap-straked in dory
fashion and proportionally somewhat greater freeboard. An occasional bateau type with arc bottom is encountered. Generally hunters
favored the round-bottom skiffs for the greater ease in "rocking off and
over" reeds, hummocks, and sand.

A variation of the bateau type was adapted to duck hunting.
Longer decks and wider covering boards provided a smaller and better
protected cockpit and larger decks for carrying decoys, "stools" in New
Jersey. Washboards are attached as in the sneakbox. Skiffs of this type
were usually used in the swamps bordering the river and not in open
waters. Later examples had an outrigger or bracket, usually on the
port side of the stern, for an outboard motor.

In years past, the gunning skiffs were sailed when long distances
were to be covered. When negotiating open water, oars were, and still
are, used. Many were adapted for using two pairs of oars. The pole
used in reeds or very shallow water was of ash or a shaved cedar sapling,
12 to 15 feet long. The usual diameter at butt end was $2\frac{1}{2}$ inches
tapering to 2 inches. Occasionally the butt diameter was three to $3\frac{1}{2}$
inches. The smaller end had three or four triangular appendages or
"toes" of oak which were riveted to the shaft to increase the purchase
on the bottom. Sometimes a spring-loaded double duckfoot device of
metal was attached to the end of the pole for the same purpose. A
paddle was usually carried and of course in recent years, an outboard
motor. The last gunning skiff was built by Joseph Myers of Fairton
about 1940. None have been built in recent years as game, unpolluted
tidelands, and fresh-water marshes diminish. The construction of these
very handsome and interesting craft is a barely remembered art.

SOURCES

Publications

Kirkbride's New Jersey Business Directory, 1850.
Talbot and Blood, *New Jersey Business Directory,* 1866.
Bishop, Nathaniel H. *Voyage of the Paper Canoe.* Boston, 1878.

Unpublished Material

New Jersey Census records, 1870.

General Descriptive, Historical, and Technical Data

L. Albertson Huber, Hydrographic Engineer, N.J. State Division of Shell Fisheries.

John Dubois, ship and boat builder of Mauricetown, former oyster boat captain.

Dr. Sherman Garrison, Bridgeton.

Lloyd Goodrich, Director Emeritus, Whitney Museum, New York.

Joseph Hancock, Hancock's Harbor.

Marty Reeves, gunning guide, of Mauricetown.

Harvey Dolbow, fisherman, of Penns Grove.

Miss Elizabeth S. Myers, Bridgeton.

Paintings by Thomas Eakins

The Artist and His Father Hunting Reed Birds. 1874 (location unknown).

Pushing for Rail. 1874. Metropolitan Museum of Art.

Starting Out After Rail. 1874. Boston Museum of Fine Arts.

Starting Out After Rail. 1874. Wichita Art Museum.

Will Schuster and Black Man Going Shooting. 1876. Stephen C. Clark Collection.

Rail Shooting. Drawing after Eakins. *Scribner's Magazine,* July 1881.

"Starting Out After Rail," by Thomas Eakins, 1874. *Courtesy of the Museum of Fine Arts, Boston, Hayden Collection.*

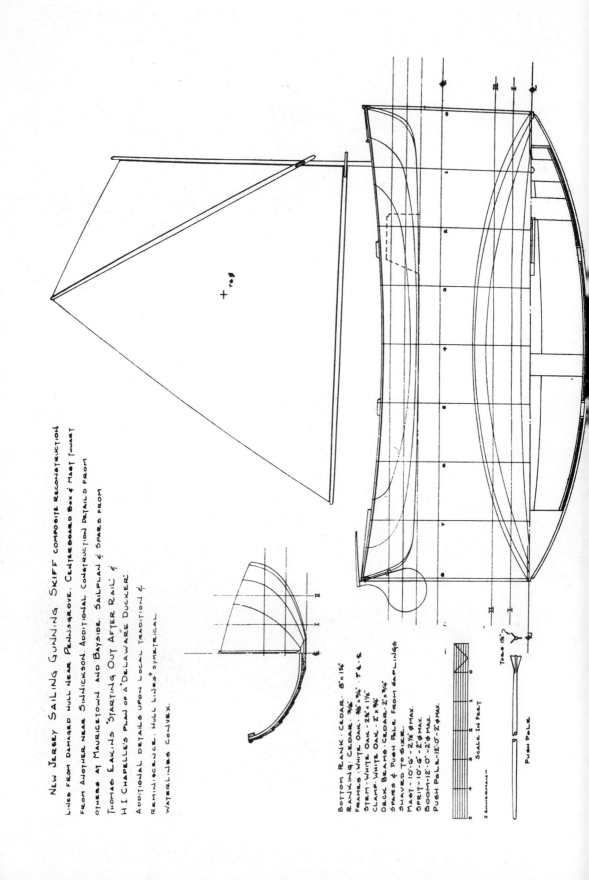

New Jersey Sailing Gunning Skiff composite reconstruction lines from damaged hull near Pennsgrove. Centerboard box & mast thwart from another near Sinnickson. Additional construction details from others at Mauricetown and Bayside. Sailplan & spars from Thomas Eakins "Starting Out After Rail" & H.I. Chapelle's plan of a "Delaware Ducker". Additional details upon local tradition & reminiscence. Hull lines symetrical waterlines convex.

Bottom plank: Cedar: 8"x1¼"
Planking: Cedar: ¾"
Frames: White oak: 16"x¾" ? & 6
Stem: White oak: 2¼x1½
Clamp: White oak: 2 x ¾
Deck beams: Cedar: 2x¾
Spars & push pole from saplings shaved to size.
Mast-10'-6" - 2½" Ø max.
Sprit-10'-6" - 2" Ø max.
Boom-12'-0" - 2" Ø max.
Push pole-12'-0" - 2" Ø max.

Scale in Feet

Push Pole

Lapstrake gunning skiff with oval cockpit, Bayside, 1967. The larger boat is a shad skiff.

Bateau type gunning skiff, c. 1920, sides ⅜-inch cedar, bottom, ½-inch cedar.

An old gunning skiff found by John DuBois at Cape May in 1968.

LAP STRAKE CONSTRUCTION

Coaming and Covering
Boards Supported on Knees

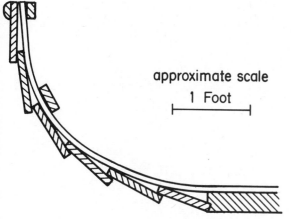

approximate scale
1 Foot

Dimensions			
covering boards	⅝ x 4	white cedar	
sides	⅜, ½ or ⅝	"	"
bottom	½ or ⅝	"	"
knees	⅝ or ¾	"	"
carlin	¾ x 1½	"	"
sheer clamp	1 x 1¼	"	"
chine	1 x 1¼	"	"
rub strake	h.r. 1¼	"	oak
coaming	½ x 3	"	"
bottom frames	¾ x 1⅛	"	"
stem, stern	1¼ x 2¼	"	"

USUAL

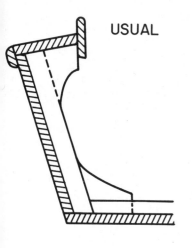

BATEAU CONSTRUCTION

UNCOMMONLY RUGGED
with carlin, sheer clamp and chine

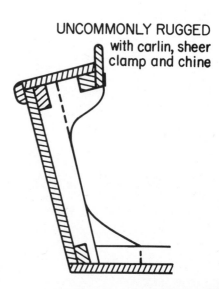

Dimensions			
coaming	⅜ x 2	white oak	
rub strake	h.r. ¾	"	"
frames	½–⅝ x ⅝–¾	"	"
covering boards	⅜	"	cedar
knees	⅝	"	"
planking	¼ – ⅝	"	"
bottom plank	¾ – ⅞	"	"

Slab-side gunning skiff at John DuBois' dock, Mauricetown, 1968. Note oars, paddle, and push poles.

Push boat.

Lap-strake, slab-side gunning skiff rigged for duck, built by
Harry Ford, Bordentown, 1968.

5

The Shrewsbury Crab Skiff

The lucrative North Jersey commercial crab fishery, and the skiff it fostered, are largely forgotten. Crabbing remains as a relaxing but only moderately productive excuse for passing an afternoon on the water.

The blue crab used to abound in the shallow bays, inlets, creeks, and rivers along the shore. The most productive were the Navesink or North Shrewsbury, the Shrewsbury, the Shark, the Manasquan, the Metedeconk, the Toms and Forked Rivers. There were many other productive waters less developed commercially. The commercial fishery was developed in the Shrewsbury and Navesink as early as 1855. In the early years, Long Branch was the center due to the large local market, large transient summer population, and reliable summer transportation by water and rail. Its success encouraged men from Long Branch to pioneer the crab fishery at Indian River, Delaware, in 1873. Other resort areas, Atlantic City and Cape May, had productive crab fisheries primarily for local consumption. Commercial crabbing had extended to the Manasquan River by 1870. Regulation was considered necessary within a few years, resulting in the passage of an act in 1874 to regulate crab fishing.

The most valuable and prized product was the soft-shelled crab or "shedder." The hard-shelled crab was also used, sometimes for bait. Crabs were caught in shallow water with a hand net. The shallow twine net was strung on an iron ring a foot in diameter, mounted on an 8-foot wood shaft. The crabber drifted in his skiff, scooping up crabs in clear water to depths to three feet. Rarely, he waded pulling a small wood lath receptacle for the crabs. The common method was the use of a baited trawl or trot line. Meat, old fish, pieces of eel or fish heads were tied to 2-foot lengths of light line. These were secured, at intervals of 2 feet, to a ½- or ¾-inch manila line 500 feet in length. The ends of the large line were fastened to light poles which could be thrust into the bottom at the selected site. The crabber pulled himself slowly back and forth along the trawl while carefully raising it from the bottom. Crabs feeding on the baits were scooped up with a hand net. In deeper water, the trot line was attached to buoys which were anchored. The trawl lines were occasionally as long as 1,200 feet. Crab traps were not usually employed. Crabs were also taken in lobster pots, gill nets, fykes, and seines but were considered a nuisance if not the object of the fisherman. Most soft crabs were taken by the scoop net as they do not actively feed in that condition. "Comers," which are about to shed, feed actively.

The three types of crab were temporarily separated in baskets in the skiff, or into towed receptacles made of laths. Specialized skiffs were built with wet wells, smack fashion. Later, the crabs were transferred to storage cars or pens.

The floating pens were introduced about 1860 and were moored in coves close to shore. They were constructed of laths or thin boards, were 4 to 8 feet square, and 1 foot deep. There was a partition which had a hinged cover. Soft crabs were packed for shipment promptly, particularly in hot weather when the new shell hardened rapidly. The freshly caught "comers" in the crab car were examined two or three times a day, the soft crabs being removed and packed for shipment as they appeared. They were very liable to injury if left with the others.

The soft crabs were packed for shipment in lath boxes 2 by 3 foot, 3 inches in depth. A layer of seaweed or salt grass was placed in the box. The crabs were very carefully and uniformily placed in the box at a slight angle to prevent movement and injury. More moist seaweed or salt grass was used between, and as a covering and padding. The boxes, holding from four to six dozen crabs, were iced for shipment during hot weather. Crabs remained alive and in good condition for several days. Hard crabs were shipped in barrels, padded with seaweed or salt grass. In 1880 soft crabs sold for 50¢ to $2.00 and hard crabs for 15¢ to 20¢ a dozen. The bulk of the crabs were marketed in New York, after the local market had been satisfied. In the Manasquan and Shark River areas, consumption by the large summer population often exhausted the available local supply.

Active crabbing started about mid-May, the first soft crabs appearing about mid-July. The season continued until late fall but hard crabs were taken all winter. During the winter, crabs moved to deeper water so that long-handled tongs were used. Winter crabbing was not very actively pursued.

In the year 1880, between Sandy Hook and Barnegat Inlet, 515 men and boys were employed in crabbing, June through September. The total catch amounted to 285,825 dozen, valued at $128,612. The value of hard crabs used as bait was $6,250. New Jersey's northern shore and adjacent shore was a leading producer of soft crabs between 1880 and 1910.

A specialized skiff was developed in the last quarter of the 19th century. It was favored by the professionals, but the common, flat-bottomed bateau, or "flat iron skiff," was also widely used. The crab skiff developed in the Shrewsbury River, the known builders being Lawrence Newman of Pleasure Bay, Abram Joralemon of Monmouth Beach, and William Seaman of Branchport. The crab skiffs at first glance resembled the ordinary flat-bottomed bateau. A closer look indicates that they had many features of the Sea Bright skiff, commonly produced by the same three builders. The general dimensions, however, were similar to the local bateau. William Seaman built the crab skiffs to fill in time between other work, and conveniently made use of shorter lengths of planking and timbers. Seaman also ran an oyster parlor, marketed shellfish, and had a boat livery which rented many of his specialized crab skiffs. He appears to have been the principal developer and builder.

The average dimensions were length 16 feet, beam 4 feet, and height amidships 15 inches. The sides flared about 20 degrees and were constructed of four, rarely five, planks. Forward sections were U-shaped, becoming prismatic farther aft, and finally ending with a flat-sided bateau transom. The frames were steam-bent white oak. The bottom was planked longitudinally of white cedar. The lap-strake sides were also white cedar. The planking and bottom were copper riveted. There was a single thwart with a parting board beneath. The short forward seat covered a small compartment and the long after seat covered multiple compartments, including two or three wet wells for the crabs. In 1900, a finished Seaman crab skiff with oars, oar locks, and anchor sold for $24. A few skiffs had a cross-planked bottom and occasionally the wet wells were under the center thwart.

The skiffs had a reputation for rowing easily, the U-shaped forward sections making for a dryer and quieter hull than the bateau.

The local crab fishery was unable to compete with those of Delaware and Chesapeake Bay, following World War I. Catches diminished and local fishermen turned to better paid employment. A few local crabbers, usually of advanced years, continued to hawk their catch from door to door until the late 1920's.

SOURCES

Publication

Report of the Fisheries Industry of the United States. G. Brown Goode. Washington, D.C., 1883. A part of the Census Report for 1880.

Anecdotal and Local Information

Harold A. Seaman, Long Branch
Edgar A. Huff, Long Branch
Joseph A. Banfield, Oakhurst
Herman Bennett, Spring Lake Heights

Views of typical Shrewsbury crab skiff.

SHREWSBURY RIVER CRAB SKIFF

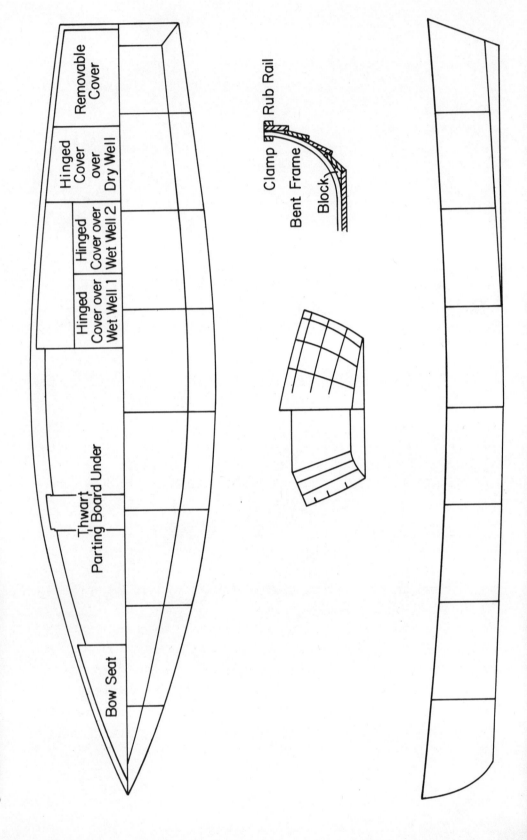

Removable Cover

Hinged Cover over Dry Well

Hinged Cover over Wet Well 2

Hinged Cover over Wet Well 1

Thwart
Parting Board Under

Bow Seat

Clamp

Rub Rail

Bent Frame

Block

6

The Raritan Bay Oyster Skiff

The formerly extensive and lucrative oyster industry of Raritan Bay has been largely forgotten. It fostered boat builders who constructed a type of skiff similar to that employed about nearby Staten Island and other areas adjacent to New York Bay.

Raritan Bay extends eastward as a triangle from an apex at Perth Amboy, for six miles toward Sandy Hook. The eastern end of the Bay is marked by Point Comfort on the south and Great Kills on Staten Island. The New Jersey oystermen were centered in Perth Amboy and in the more advantageously situated Keyport along the Bay's southern shore. Perth Amboy had a population of 10,000 in 1880 when its oyster industry had begun to decline.

An act was passed in 1824 to encourage and regulate the planting of oysters in the Township of Perth Amboy. Oyster planting was well established by 1840, supplying mainly local, and some more distant markets, in the next half century. By 1860 there were six planters who employed twenty-nine hands and used seed oysters from Newark Bay and Virginia. They produced and marketed 23,500 bushels of "Princess Bay" oysters valued at $19,500. In 1880 the planting grounds of 300 acres extended for a mile southeast by south from Ferry Point. There were other lesser beds. The average depth in the major bed was five feet, less in the others. The beds were staked out by individual planters before seeding with young oysters. In these waters, the optimum period of growth before harvesting was three years. Longer periods produced the larger, more profitable "box" oyster. The smaller "cullen" was used locally. The "box" size were valued at $7 and the "cullen" at $3.00 per thousand in 1880.

Oysters intended for fall marketing were raised by tonging from the soft muddy bottom grounds and were then shifted to firmer sandy or gravelly bottoms during March, April, and May. This move aided in producing a symmetrical, strong shelled, meaty, flavorful oyster when harvested in September, October, and November. After being tonged from the bottom, they were rough-culled immediately in the skiff. They were transferred to the skiff tenders, small sloops or catboats owned by the proprietors or planters. The oysters were transported to floats immediately. The floats were barge-like, barely afloat, with perforated sides to expose the oysters to the waters free of contact with the bottom. The floats were moored most commonly in the brackish waters of the Rahway River to "drink" the oysters. Exposure to at least one tide was required. The water of less salinity caused the oyster to rid itself of sand, grit, and other extraneous matter. It also induced fluid retention by the oyster, "fattening" it for market.

When the soft bottom grounds were vacated in the spring by the transfer operation, they were promptly replanted. The seed oysters were obtained from the natural beds in the lower Raritan River a few miles upstream, or from other sources. Significant production in the Perth Amboy area was ended by 1900 due to increasing pollution and encroachment on the beds by dredged channels for the increasingly deep vessels.

The center of the Perth Amboy oyster industry was at the foot of Gordon Street. Most related business was carried on in the area of Gordon Street between Water and Front Streets. It extended along Front from Gordon to Eagleswood Avenue. Most of the small sailing craft of the oyster fleet, and many of the skiffs, used Woglom's and Sofield's docks in this area. The latter was a nearly enclosed area affording maximum protection. A short distance south was White's dock, also used by the oyster fleet. Among the oyster planters were members of the Woglom and Sofield families, C. White, H. A. Drost, and Robert Seaman.

Keyport, the other oyster center, had a population of 3,500 in 1880. It was also the marine terminus for much local transport and a ship- and boat-building center. The oyster planting grounds covered 1,600 acres between the town and Princess Bay on Staten Island. Other areas farther east were entirely in New Jersey and covered a total of 25,000 acres. Closely adjacent areas were clam grounds, adding to the continuing friction, and competition for bottom grounds, between clammer and oysterman.

The Keyport grounds had a water depth varying from two to sixteen feet. Methods were similar to those employed at Perth Amboy. Seed was obtained from the natural beds in the Raritan River, Newark Bay, Arthur Kill, and occasionally as far away as the Chesapeake or Long Island. The pioneer oystermen were Capt. Peter Metzger, Jacob and Benjamin Decker, and Cornelius Britton, who established themselves between 1840 and 1844. They had formerly been proprietors in Staten Island oystering. In 1860 there were fourteen planters, each with from two to ten employees. The annual production of the individual planters varied in value from $1,400 to $18,000. By 1880 there were twenty-three planters and eighty-nine hands. Twenty of the latter were Negroes, chiefly from Virginia.

In addition to the sloops, catboats, and skiffs used at Perth Amboy, there were small scows and flat-bottomed bateaus. The process of "drinking" the oysters was done in lower Luppatcong or Keyport Creek, to a lesser extent in lower Matawan and Chingarora Creeks.

In 1902 there were twenty-three planters and the annual product was valued at $250,000. The fishery in 1904 had fourteen lessees of planting grounds, the individual plots ranging from six to 140 acres and averaging about thirty acres. By 1907 the lessees had increased to seventeen and the plots varied from two and one half to 166 acres. In the later years, sale of oysters in the shell was increasingly replaced by shucked oysters sold in three- and five-gallon cans.

The center for the Keyport industry was about lower Luppatcong

Creek. Most small sailing craft were moored along the shore and bulk-heads between the mouth and the Front Street bridge. Small buildings related to oystering, and later shucking houses, were mostly north of the bridge and close by the creek. Skiffs, floats, and other craft were moored or beached within a short distance upstream of the bridge. Activities also extended west along Front Street to the lower end of Broadway, and to Cuttrell's shipyard on Brown's Point, at the lower end of Broadway. Among the oyster planters were members of the Britton family, Thomas S. Brown, Jeremiah Huff, and James Camp-bell, all residing in the immediate area.

Operations continued to the beginning of World War I, the last major planter being the J. and J. W. Ellsworth Co. They commonly employed Lond Island seed in the later years. Their close Long Island ties resulted in eventual removal there. The Ellsworth shucking house was built about 1900 on the south side of West Front Street, just east of the creek. It was managed by A. S. Van Buskirk until oystering ceased following World War I. The building is still there. Very limited, sporadic, and possibly illegal operations were carried on for a short time afterward.

The oyster tonging skiff for Raritan Bay was built to meet the particular needs of the oysterman in that area. They are identical, or similar, to oyster skiffs used in similar situations in the waters of New York Bay. We fortunately have an excellent description of these in an 1880 report on the shipbuilding industry and a set of lines with brief descriptive notes published in 1906. Additional data are furnished by a photograph taken in 1908, by lines from a half hull, and the descriptions of a few old oystermen and boat builders.

Henry Hall, the compiler of the 1880 report, says that 125 oyster skiffs could be seen off Perth Amboy and gathering about their landing places on both sides of the Kill. They were produced by two or three boat shops, one builder with an assistant producing twenty in a year. Each boat needed about 250 feet of cedar for planking and flooring. The cost of each boat was $90 to $100. The boats are regularly framed and have a flat bottom tapering to a point at each end. The clinker-built sides are copper riveted to the frames which are on 20-inch centers. The sides are full and round and the stern perpendicular but V-shaped, as in a yawl. The boats come in three sizes, 18-, 19- and 20-foot. This is the length of the bottom, overall length being 4 to 4½ feet more. The beam is about 6 feet and depth 20 to 22 inches. The planking is pine or cedar. The frames are of roots of white oak, selected as having the proper natural curvature, squared and fitted to their places. The bottom is floored over and the thwarts made removable permitting a large pile of oysters to lay amidships. Most skiffs have a mast with small fore-and-aft sail, the mast being placed a little forward of amidships, but not in the bow. There is generally a centerboard when there is a sail.

The 1906 description and lines appear in *Forest and Stream* magazine. Some construction details, differing from the previous account, are given. The skiffs are described as very steady, even when deeply loaded, not apt to be swamped. They were frequently fitted with a narrow dagger board and a small spritsail, and were very fair sailers.

The skiffs were described as single or double, depending on the number of thwarts for rowers. The double skiffs were usually 24 feet overall. During the later years about Keyport, most skiffs were about 20 feet, smaller than those previously described by Hall.

The sketch at the end of this chapter indicates some of the details of construction and scantlings. There were notable variations including the use of jogged frames in some very well built boats and the eventual substitution of bent for sawn frames in the smaller and more recent skiffs. There are no skiffs of New Jersey construction surviving although there are a few boats of similar type preserved in museums.

The recognized builders were John E. Halstead, William Cuttrell, and William L. Force of Keyport; Jacob Hadden, John P. Woglom, William Ferguson, and Richard Kingsland of Perth Amboy. Another probable builder was William Clark of Port Monmouth. The builders named covered a span from before 1870 to after 1900. There were undoubtedly other recognized builders and some who were occasional builders, primarily for themselves.

The similarities of the oyster skiff, the Sea Bright skiff, and some examples of the Whitehall skiff are evident. These are lap-strake construction, raking transom stern, general proportions and planked-up skeg. A very similar British cousin must be viewed with the same eye. This is the Aldeburgh sprat boat; a transom stern, lap-strake, sailing beach skiff, usually 15 feet in length. The historical and generic relationship of these small craft, the 18th century ship's boat, and the colonial bateau of the French and Indian War are unknown. Their common features are evident.

SOURCES

Publications

Report of the Ship-Building Industry of the United States. Henry Hall, Special Agent. Washington, 1882–3. A part of the Census Report for 1880.

"The Oyster-Industry." Robert Ingersoll. Washington, D.C., 1881. A part of the report on the fishery industries in the Census Report for 1880.

"Notes on the Oyster Industry of New Jersey." Ansley Hall. In *Report of the U.S. Commission of Fish and Fisheries.* Part XVIII. Washington, 1894.

Reports of the New Jersey Commissioners of Fisheries, Shell Fisheries and Oyster Commissions. Various years.

Historical and Biographical Atlas of New Jersey Coast. Woolman & Rose. Philadelphia, 1878.

New Historical Atlas of Middlesex County. Evarts & Stewart. Philadelphia, 1876.

Atlas of Monmouth County, N.J. Beers, Comstock & Kline. New York, 1873.

State Atlas of New Jersey. Beers, Comstock & Kline. New York, 1872.

"Lines of Oyster Skiff." Martin C. Erismann. *Forest and Stream.* February 24. 1906.

Unpublished Material

Photograph of oyster skiff with culling board. 1908.

Lines of oyster skiff from half hull, circa 1900.

Anecdotal and Local Information

Louis Booz, Perth Amboy

Damon Heyer, Keyport

George Walling, Keyport

Charles Applegate, Keyport

Miss Vera Conover, Keyport

Miss J. Mabel Brown, Keyport

I am particularly indebted to Mr. John Kochiss, research associate, The Marine Historical Association, Mystic Seaport, for historical citations.

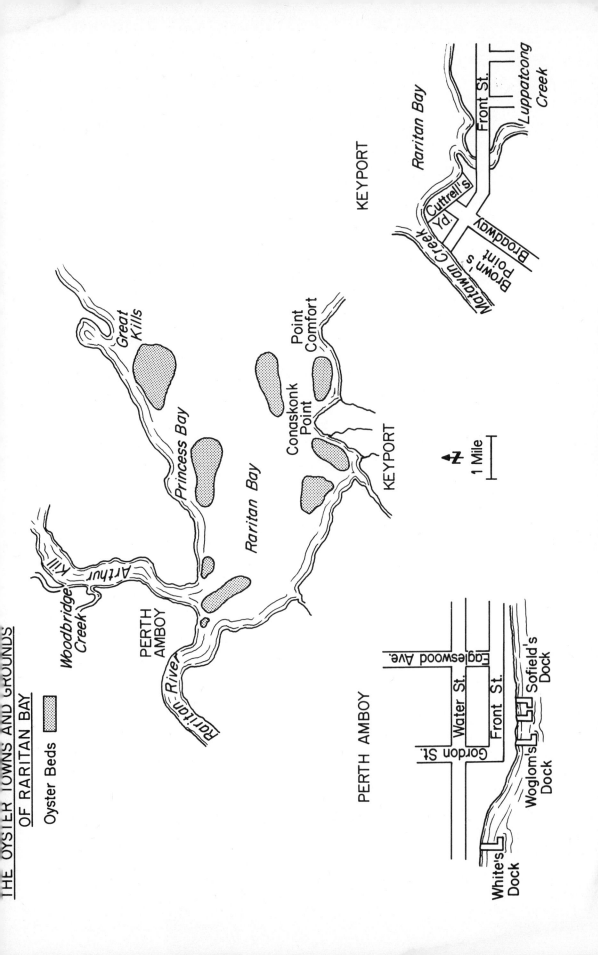

THE OYSTER TOWNS AND GROUNDS
OF RARITAN BAY

Oyster Beds

Woodbridge Creek

Arthur Kill

Raritan River

PERTH AMBOY

Princess Bay

Great Kills

Raritan Bay

Conaskonk Point

Point Comfort

KEYPORT

1 Mile

N

Matawan Creek

Cuttrell's Yd.

Brown's Point

Broadway

Front St.

Raritan Bay

Luppatcong Creek

KEYPORT

PERTH AMBOY

Gordon St.

Water St.

Eagleswood Ave.

Front St.

White's Dock

Woglom's Dock

Sofield's Dock

OYSTER SKIFF CONSTRUCTION

ALTERNATE
Second strake doubled
with cap board

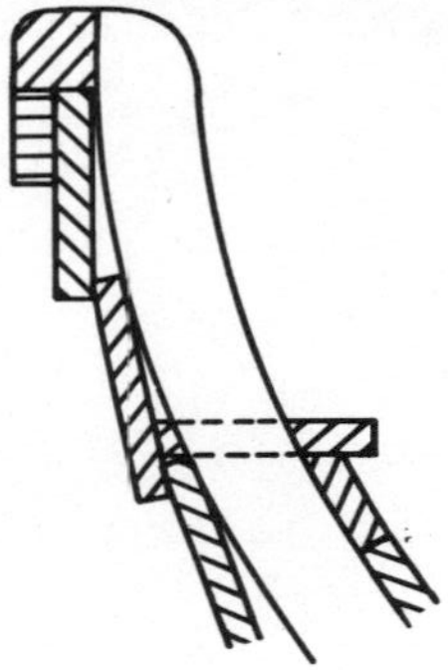

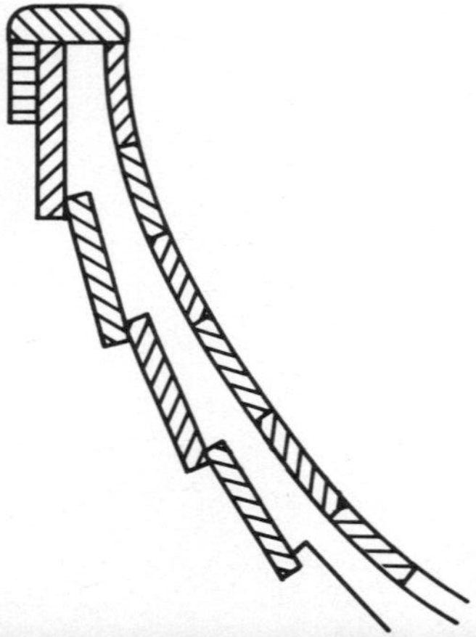

RECENT
Bent frames as in Sea Bright skiff.
In smaller sizes only.

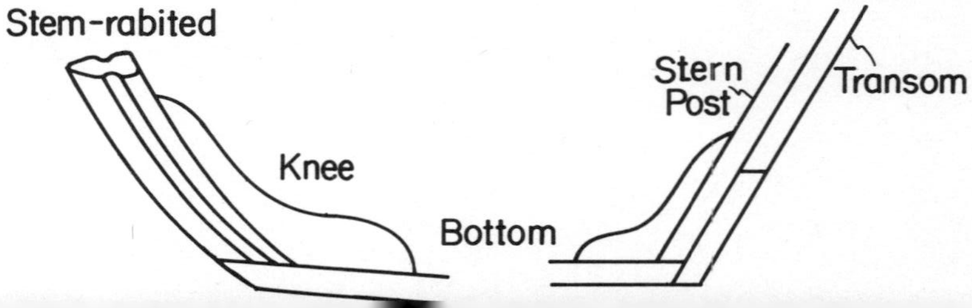

Stem-rabited

Knee

Bottom

Stern Post

Transom

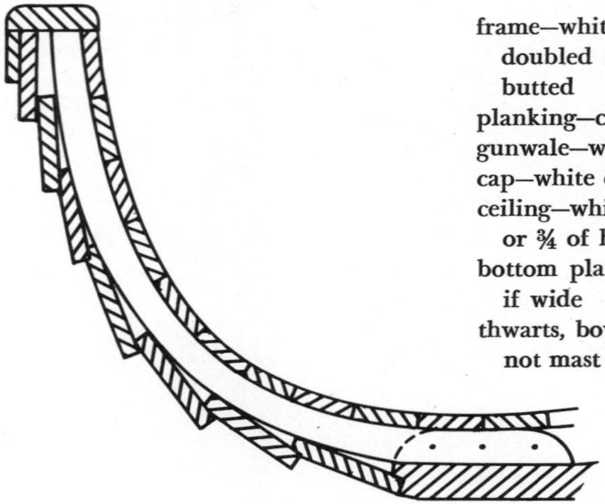

frame—white oak sawn, 1¼″, width 1½–2½″,
doubled at bottom except at ends where
butted

planking—cedar ¾–⅞″

gunwale—white oak ¾″

cap—white oak ¾″

ceiling—white pine or cedar ¾″, in center ⅝
or ¾ of hull

bottom plank—yellow pine 1¼–1½″, splined
if wide

thwarts, bow & stern platforms movable, but
not mast thwart

USUAL

RARE
Jogged frames

OYSTER SKIFF

from half hull, Keyport
18 X 25 5/16", scale unknown

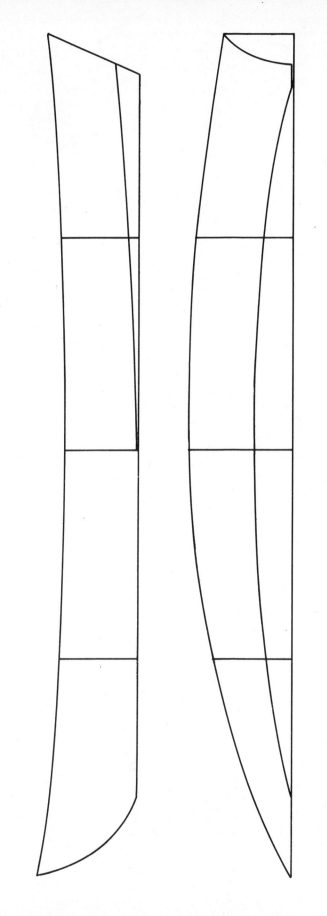
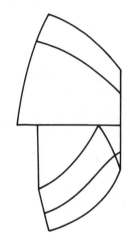

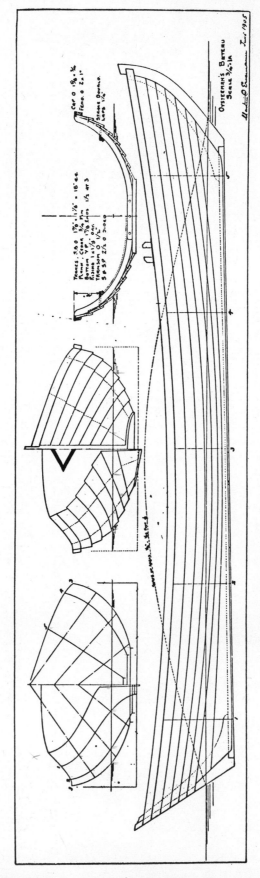

Oysterman's bateau, drawn by Martin C. Erismann, in *Forest and Stream*, February 24, 1906.

Oyster skiff with culling board on exhibit at the Mariners Museum. *Courtesy of the Mariners Museum.*

Luppatcong Creek south of Front Street, Keyport, about 1900. The J. and J. W. Elsworth shucking plant is in the background. In the foreground are oyster flats and tonging skiffs. *Courtesy of Vera Conover.*

Luppatcong Creek north of Front Street. Oyster flat in foreground. *Courtesy of Vera Conover.*

Two oyster sloops frozen in off Keyport, 1890. *Courtesy of Vera Conover.*

A catboat under sail, oyster sloops and a power dredge in background, Keyport, 1890. *Courtesy of Vera Conover.*

Fig. 1.

Fig. 2.

THE OYSTER INDUSTRY.

Fig. 1. Inclosed dock for oyster-vessels at Perth Amboy, N. J.   (Sect. v, vol. ii, p. 546.)
Fig. 2. "The Creek" at Keyport, N. J., with oyster-boats, skiffs, and scows.   (Sect. v, vol. ii, p. 546.)

Drawings by Ernest Ingersoll.

From *Fishing Industry of the U.S.*, George Brown Goode, Washington, D.C., 1887.

PLATE 238.

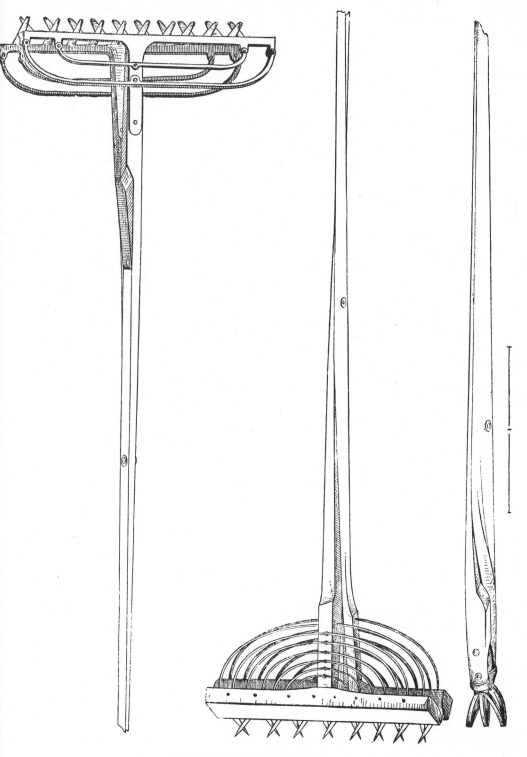

THE OYSTER INDUSTRY.

Oyster tongs and nippers.   (Sect. v, vol. ii, p. 551.)

From *Fishing Industry of the U.S.*, George Brown Goode, Washington, D.C., 1887.

Oyster skiff with culling board. New Jersey Report of the Bureau of Shell Fisheries, 1908.

7

Other Gunning Skiffs

The great tidal marshes of New Jersey were the habitat of vast numbers of waterfowl, which for centuries were an attraction to hunters. Formerly, the valleys of the Passaic, Hackensack, and Raritan Rivers, Arthur Kill, and the streams and creeks entering them, were active hunting fields. The increase in population, pollution of all types, and drainage of tidelands has left a rapidly diminishing area still fit for fish, waterfowl, and the men who follow them. The remaining wetlands are along the coast south of Sandy Hook and along the lower Delaware. This region is rapidly being drained, polluted, suburbanized, and debeautified.

A number of gunning skiff types were devised. The Barnegat sneakbox and the rail gunning skiffs are covered in other chapters. Other variant and less common types were also used, and are the subject of this chapter.

The general requirements of a gunning skiff are to an extent contradictory. It must be small enough to be rowed or sailed easily by one man, light enough to be beached or hefted over obstructions by one man, but large enough to carry the hunter and his gear with comfort and safety. The equipment of the wild-fowler includes decoys or "stool ducks" in substantial numbers, two and a half dozen at a minimum, gun, shells, food, drink, occasionally a small stove and adequate clothing. The required warm clothing established one of the dimensions of the skiff. To keep feet warm, at least two pairs of heavy socks must be worn under boots. This results in a foot length of 12 inches in the average gunner, and frequently much more. In order to keep one's feet under the deck in comfort and to permit ordinary movement, there must be a minimum of 14 inches clearance between floorboards and deck. Other requirements are sufficient seaworthiness to meet local weather conditions, mechanical strength to allow it to be hauled over obstructions, and metal wear strips for protection against ice. There may be peculiar local needs such as adaptability to use in narrow creeks or drainage ditches, and many others. Commonly the requirements have been met by a skiff 12 feet long, 4 feet beam and a depth of hull of 16 inches. The cockpit is 2½ by 4 feet with parallel sides, raised coaming, and a cover which is frequently hinged in the center for ease in stowing. Rowlocks were pivoted so they could be folded flat with the deck. An additional low three-sided coaming was fastened to the deck outboard, about the after half of the sides and across the stern. These washboards were provided to stow decoys and game outside the narrow confines of the hull. There is often a folding canvas spray and wind screen at the forward end of the deck.

A bateau type was used in the Mullica River area and adjacent waters. This was low-sided, flat-bottomed, with slightly flaring sides and a high deck camber. There were no provisions for sailing in the examples seen. The central cockpit is rather small and the deck long. There were no provisons for an outboard motor but there were folding rowlocks. A similar boat was provided with a single lee-board bracket but was powered by an outboard motor. All those examined were built of cedar planking over oak frames.

Another bateau type was employed about Tuckerton, and also in the far western side of Burlington County on the Delaware. This was similar in size and construction to the first but was higher sided, had more flaring sides, a daggerboard and a mast step. The size and shape of spars, board, rudder and rig is unknown.

The garvey has been developed as a gunning skiff. The same general dimensions of 12 by 4 feet are usual, although a few examples were seen as small as 10½ by 3½ feet. This is due to the comparatively greater displacement of a hull of this shape. Some of the garvey boxes are roughly built, with high sides and flat decks. The better built examples have lower sides and a cambered deck. At least one older example was extremely well and carefully constructed, had a dagger-board and mast.

The garvey boxes are usually planked with white cedar over white oak frames. Bottoms are usually cross planked. Cockpit and wash-boards are similar to the other gunning skiffs. Some later models were constructed of marine plywood. One V-bottom model was planked across in the forward quarter of the bottom but longitudinally in the flat after three quarters. Other V models had a constant deadrise and longitudinal planking.

A variation of the garvey type featured low sides and sharply slop-ing covering boards at an angle of 45 degrees to the sides. These "ditch boxes" were designed to negotiate narrow waterways. The cockpit was sufficiently long to accommodate two gunners. There were hand rails for lifting, along the sloping sides. Propulsion was by pole, oars, or an outboard motor. In some of this type, the sharply sloped deck sides ran the whole length, but usually ended at a foredeck a quarter the length of the hull. Construction is similar to the previous.

Another type was the melonseed. There are no existing local ex-amples and none are recollected by the dozen or so guides and gunning skiff builders questioned. Many of these men were of advanced years. It is probable that the melonseed passed out of existence by the turn of the century. The builders acquainted with them owed their knowl-edge to the excellent plan reproduced in H. I. Chappelle's *American Small Sailing Craft*. This in turn has been upon an unpublished draw-ing from the files of *Forest and Stream* magazine about 1888. Two half-hulls of very similar type have been examined. One is identified by the name "Cranmer" inscribed in pencil, an honored name in the central Barnegat Bay region. Three members are recorded as boat builders, Richard at Manahawkin about 1860, John at Tuckerton about 1866, and Samuel P. at West Creek about 1873. H. W. Cranmer was a West Creek sailmaker about 1867. One of the half-hulls is 14 by 2⅜ inches, equivalent to a boat 14 feet by 4 feet 9 inches, at a scale of 1 inch to the foot. There is a slight deck sheer, low sides, flat, tapered plank keel. The stem is curved, transom sharply sloped with a planked-up skeg. The midsection has a flat, rising floor and curved, slack, bilge. The entrance is hollow. The melonseed was apparently adapted for sailing the wider waters but their numbers were small, utility not obvious, and survival short. A confusing note is added by the habit of many gunners who refer to the sneakbox gunning skiff as a "melonseed."

A drawing of a melonseed is reproduced from the collection of Mr. Wayne P. Yarnall. The hull lines are the same as those taken from the *Cranmer* half hull. This skiff was 15 feet 8½ inches by 5 feet 6¾ inches. It was built at Absecon Island, now Atlantic City, about 1891. It has a conventional centerboard and the rudder is equipped with a tiller. The drawing from W. P. Stephens of *Rudder* magazine, reproduced in H. I. Chappelle's book is somewhat smaller, has a daggerboard, and steers by means of tiller lines.

Gunners considered any of the flat-bottom, and some of the flat-sided, gunning skiffs noisy and wet underway and noisy when moored. The smallest wave caused a slapping sound more annoying to the gunner than alarming to game. There were a number of designs which were basically garveys with sneakbox features and of course sneakboxes with low flat sides and of modified garvey construction. It is possible to categorize them only as of composite and variant type.

Gunning skiff construction is becoming a lost art. At present they are still built by Carl Adams of Nacote Creek, Gus Hinrichs of New Gretna, Reuben Corlies of Manahawkin, and Allan Chadwick of Barnegat. The aggregate age of the first three is well over the two century mark. Chadwick still constructs the classical Barnegat sneakbox type, using century old templates, while the others favor an excellent, individual, variant type. Prior to 1941 there were about two dozen recognized, although by no means fully occupied, builders of gunning skiffs. It is probable that waterfowl shooting, and therefore gunning skiff construction, will be only history in New Jersey before many years.

SOURCE

Local Information

Robert Warner, Atlantic City

Bateau type gunning skiff, low sides.

Bateau type sailing gunning skiff.

Garvey gunning box.

Ditch box.

OTHER GUNNING SKIFFS

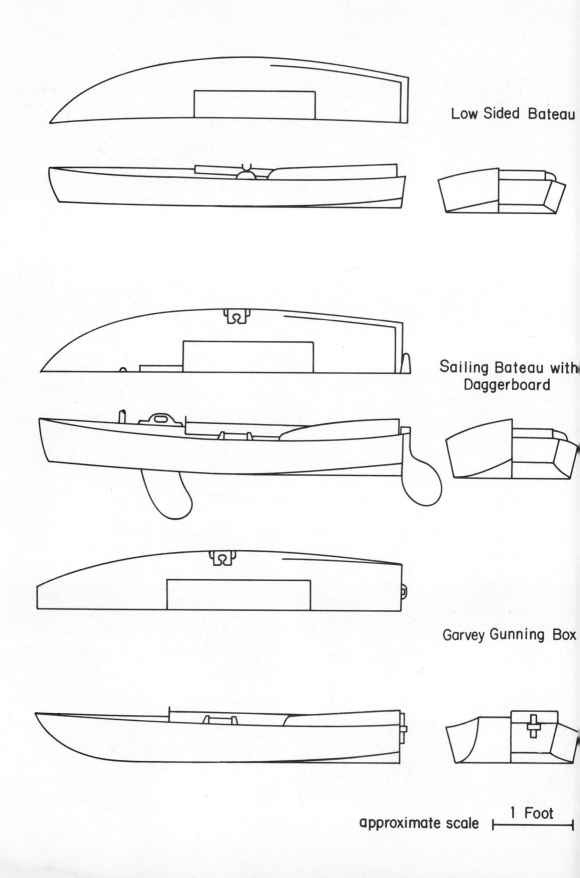

Low Sided Bateau

Sailing Bateau with
Daggerboard

Garvey Gunning Box

approximate scale ⊢———⊣ 1 Foot

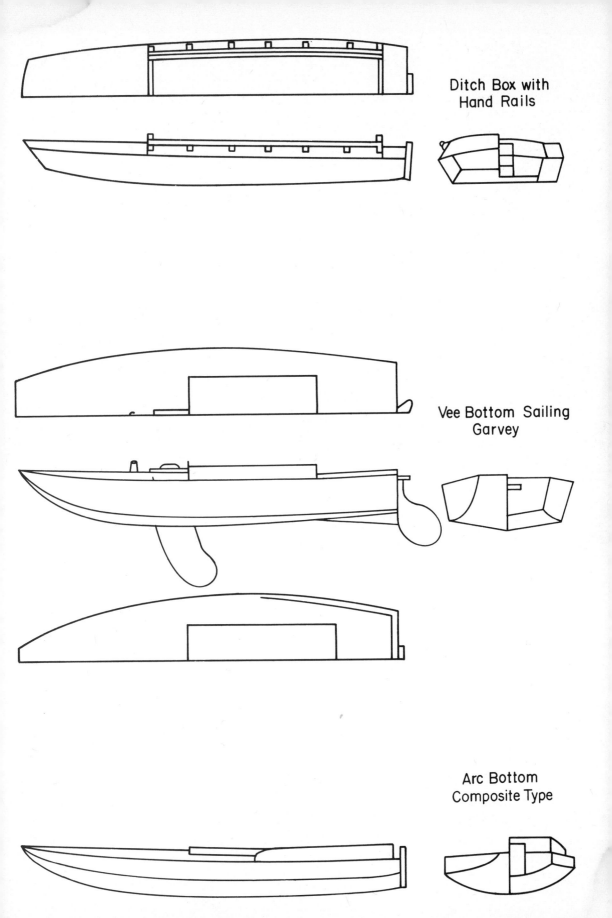

Ditch Box with
Hand Rails

Vee Bottom Sailing
Garvey

Arc Bottom
Composite Type

GUNNING SKIFF ROWLOCKS

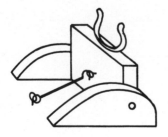

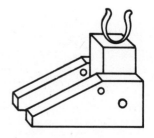

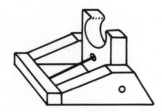

approximate scale
6 Inches

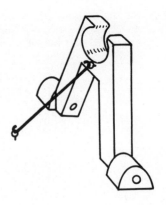

Traditional gaff-rigged gunning sneakbox built by Bartine Clayton of Silverton about 1910. *Courtesy of Thomas H. Donnelly.*

Modern gunning sneakbox of composite type, built by Gus Hinrichs for outboard power. *Courtesy of Edmond N. Skinner.*

Glossary

BATTEN—a thin strip of wood used to cover joints between planks; a thin strip of wood used to fair a curve.

BREAST HOOK—a horizontal knee to reinforce the bow of a boat.

BULKHEAD—a transverse partition in a boat or ship.

BUTT BLOCK—a short block used to reinforce the end joint between two planks.

CAULKING—material used to make the joint between two planks watertight.

CARLIN—a short fore-and-aft beam running beside a hatch, deck opening, or trunk cabin.

CARVEL (PLANKING)—planking of a hull laid side to side to present a smooth exterior.

CEILING—a lining applied to the interior of the frames of a boat or ship.

CHINE—a longitudinal angular intersection between flat exterior hull surfaces.

CHOCK—a wood or metal fitting acting as a fairlead for a rope, chain, or cable.

CLAMP—a horizontal timber secured to the inner sides of the frames in a longitudinal direction.

COAMING—raised border around a deck opening or cockpit.

CODWADS—a floor timber extending below a frame.

COVERING BOARD—a narrow deck around the cockpit of a small boat.

DEADRISE—angle between the bottom of a vessel and a horizontal plane, at the widest part of the hull.

DEADWOOD—a reinforcing piece between keel and stem piece.

DECK—a horizontal surface in a boat or ship.

FILLER BLOCK—a wood segment to fill a void, usually between the planking and clamp, between frames.

FLICH SAWN—a log sawn completely across into planks, including the bark at the edges.

FLOOR (TIMBER)—transverse framing members at the bottom of the hull.

FRAME—transverse rib-like structures to which the planking is attached.

FREEBOARD—the distance between the water and the top of the hull sides.

FYKE—a bag shaped fish trap suspended on hoops.

GARBOARD, BOX—the skeg-like appendage formed of a bottom plank and two lateral triangular fillet planks.

GARBOARD (STRAKE)—the first plank on each side of the keel. In large skiffs there may be a "second" garboard, which is a paradox.

GILL NET—a vertical net with mesh size designed to catch fish by their gills.

GUDGEON—a socket attached to the stern, to receive the pintle of a rudder.

GUNWALE—the upper edge of the side of a hull.

HALF GIRTH—the circumference of a hull from keel to sheer.

HARPING—a curved horizontal beam where deck and side planking are fastened.

HORN TIMBER—a timber attached to the sternpost, to support an overhanging stern.

KEEL—the principal longitudinal backbone of a hull.

KEELSON—an auxiliary longitudinal reinforcing member.

KNEE—a knee shaped reinforcing member between two intersecting structures.

KNUCKLE—a triangular block inserted into the void between a frame and lap strake plank.

LAP STRAKE—a method of hull planking in which each plank overlaps the next plank by a short distance.

LUTING—thin packing material to make a longitudinal seam waterproof.

MOLD—a transverse form which determines hull shape.

PARTING BOARD—a board or plank placed vertically on a deck to separate or contain fish.

PINTLE—a pin-like metal fitting on a rudder which fits into a gudgeon on the stern.

PLANK KEEL—a flat horizontal center plank.

POUND NET—a system of nets forming an enclosure.

RABBET—a longitudinal recess forming an interior angle. Usually to receive a matching piece.

RELIEVING PORT—an aperture in a hull or coaming to permit egress of water.

RUB STRAKE—a longitudinal exterior timber to take up wear or protect against injury.

SCANTLING—cross section size of framing members.

SCARF—a tapered end joint between longitudinal members.

SEINE NET—a vertical net suspended between weights at the bottom and floats at the top.

SHEATHING—an outer protective layer on a hull.

SHEER CLAMP—longitudinal timber attached to the inside of the frames at the top of the hull.

SHEER STRAKE—the top plank of a hull.

SHEER—the fore and aft curve of the deck, or top of the hull.

SHELF—horizontal, longitudinal member.

SHIPLAP—boards, jointed by longitudinal rabbets to form a smooth surface.

SKEG—a short longitudinal vertical appendage to the after end of a hull.

SKIFF—a small, light rowing or sailing boat.

SOLE PLANK—protective sheathing applied to the bottom of a hull.

SPLINE—a narrow strip inserted into the edges of adjacent planks to join them.

SPRIT SAIL—a roughly quadrilateral sail, a corner of which is supported by a light oblique spar (sprit).

STEM—an unright member into which the sides are joined, forming the bow.

STERN POST—an upright member into which the after end of the planking is attached, forming the stern.

STRAKE—a plank, or continuous course of planks forming the hull shell.

STRINGER—a longitudinal strengthening member of the hull, fastened to the inside of the frames.

SURF BOAT—boats of various design, for launching from a beach, through surf.

THWART—a transverse horizontal seat.

THWART KNEE—a horizontal or vertical reinforcing member at the ends of a thwart.

THWART RISER—a longitudinal member on which the ends of the thwarts are fastened.

TILLER—a horizontal bar attached to a rudder, to turn the rudder.

TRANSOM—the flat after termination of a hull.

TUCK (STRAKE)—the second hull plank on a skiff of rolled garboard design. The reverse chine aft is formed by the angle between the garboard and tuck. In very large hulls, the garboard may be formed of two planks, in which case the tuck may be the third plank.

Index